JEFFREY SELLER   SANDER JACOBS   JILL FURMAN

AND

THE PUBLIC THEATER

PRESENT

H★MILTON

AN AMERICAN MUSICAL

BOOK, MUSIC AND LYRICS BY

LIN-MANUEL MIRANDA

INSPIRED BY THE BOOK *ALEXANDER HAMILTON* BY
RON CHERNOW

WITH

DAVEED DIGGS   RENÉE ELISE GOLDSBERRY   JONATHAN GROFF   CHRISTOPHER JACKSON
JASMINE CEPHAS JONES   LIN-MANUEL MIRANDA   JAVIER MUÑOZ   LESLIE ODOM, JR.
OKIERIETE ONAODOWAN   ANTHONY RAMOS   PHILLIPA SOO
AND
CARLEIGH BETTIOL   ANDREW CHAPPELLE   ARIANA DEBOSE   ALYSHA DESLORIEUX
SYDNEY JAMES HARCOURT   NEIL HASKELL   SASHA HUTCHINGS   THAYNE JASPERSON
STEPHANIE KLEMONS   MORGAN MARCELL   EMMY RAVER-LAMPMAN
JON RUA   AUSTIN SMITH   SETH STEWART   BETSY STRUXNESS
EPHRAIM SYKES   VOLTAIRE WADE-GREENE

SCENIC DESIGN	COSTUME DESIGN	LIGHTING DESIGN	SOUND DESIGN
DAVID KORINS	PAUL TAZEWELL	HOWELL BINKLEY	NEVIN STEINBERG

HAIR AND WIG DESIGN	MUSIC COORDINATOR	PRESS REPRESENTATIVE
CHARLES G. LAPOINTE	MICHAEL KELLER MICHAEL AARONS	SAM RUDY MEDIA RELATIONS

TECHNICAL SUPERVISION	PRODUCTION STAGE MANAGER	COMPANY MANAGER
HUDSON THEATRICAL ASSOCIATES	J. PHILIP BASSETT	BRIG BERNEY

CASTING	ARRANGEMENTS	GENERAL MANAGEMENT
TELSEY + COMPANY BETHANY KNOX, CSA	ALEX LACAMOIRE LIN-MANUEL MIRANDA	BASELINE THEATRICAL ANDY JONES

MUSIC DIRECTION AND ORCHESTRATIONS BY

ALEX LACAMOIRE

CHOREOGRAPHY BY

ANDY BLANKENBUEHLER

DIRECTED BY

THOMAS KAIL

THE WORLD PREMIERE OF HAMILTON WAS PRESENTED IN NEW YORK IN FEBRUARY 2015 BY THE PUBLIC THEATER.
OSKAR EUSTIS, ARTISTIC DIRECTOR   PATRICK WILLINGHAM, EXECUTIVE DIRECTOR

The purchase, rental or use of these materials does not constitute a license to perform this play.
Performance without a license is a violation of United States copyright law and
an actionable federal offense.

ISBN 978-1-4950-6988-8

EXCLUSIVELY DISTRIBUTED BY

HAL•LEONARD® CORPORATION

7777 W. BLUEMOUND RD. P.O. BOX 13819 MILWAUKEE, WI 53213

In Australia Contact:
Hal Leonard Australia Pty. Ltd.
4 Lentara Court
Cheltenham, Victoria, 3192 Australia
Email: ausadmin@halleonard.com.au

Visit Hal Leonard Online at
www.halleonard.com

Lin-Manuel Miranda is an Emmy, Grammy, and Tony Award-winning composer, lyricist, and performer, and a 2015 MacArthur Foundation Award recipient. *Hamilton*, for which he wrote the book, music and lyrics in addition to originating the title role, opened on Broadway in 2015 following a sold-out run at New York's Public Theater. Its Original Broadway Cast Recording won the 2016 Grammy Award for Best Musical Theater Album. Off-Broadway, *Hamilton* received a record-breaking 10 Lortel Awards, 3 Outer Critic Circle Awards, 8 Drama Desk Awards, the New York Drama Critics Circle Award for Best New Musical, and an OBIE for Best New American Play. Material from the show was previewed at the White House during its first-ever Evening of Poetry & Spoken Word in 2009.

Miranda's first Broadway musical, *In the Heights*, received four 2008 Tony Awards (Best Score, Best Orchestrations, Best Choreography and Best Musical), as well as Miranda's nomination for Best Leading Actor in a Musical. The show won a 2009 Grammy for its Original Broadway Cast Album and was recognized as a Finalist for the 2009 Pulitzer Prize in Drama.

Miranda is the co-composer and co-lyricist of Broadway's *Bring It On: The Musical* (2013 Tony nomination for Best Musical; 2013 Drama Desk nomination for Best Lyrics in a Musical). He contributed new songs to the revival of Stephen Schwartz' *Working*, as well as Spanish translations for the 2009 Broadway Revival of *West Side Story*.

Miranda won an Emmy Award as the lyricist of the 2013 Tony Awards opening number, "Bigger." He is the co-founder of the hip-hop improv group Freestyle Love Supreme. Miranda is the recipient of the ASCAP Foundation's Richard Rodgers New Horizons Award and the National Arts Club Medal of Honor. A graduate of Wesleyan University, he lives in New York City with his wife, son, and dog.

Special thanks to:

Jonny Baird

Nolan Bonvouloir

Brian Barone

Kurt Crowley

Khiyon Hursey

Adam Michael Kaufman

Madeline Myers

Scott Wasserman

Ian Weinberger

Will Wells

Rachael Ziering

ALEXANDER HAMILTON

Words and Music by
LIN-MANUEL MIRANDA

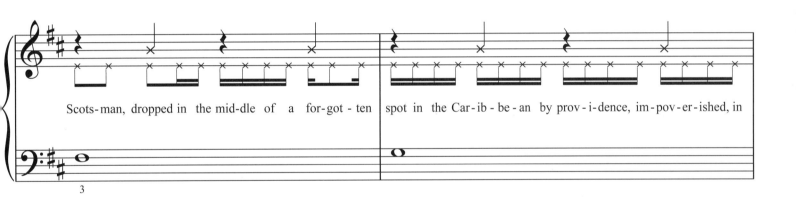

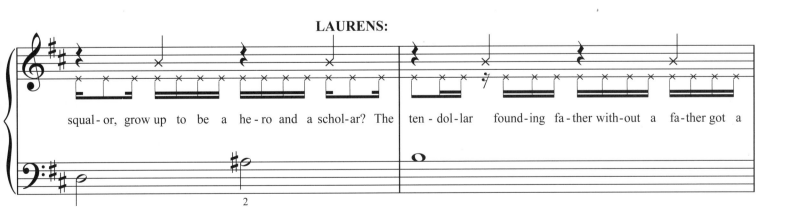

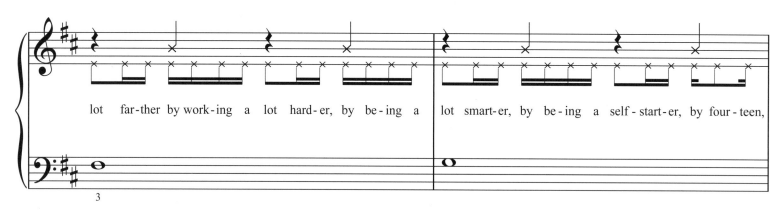

lot far-ther by work-ing a lot hard-er, by be-ing a lot smart-er, by be-ing a self-start-er, by four-teen,

JEFFERSON: Bm

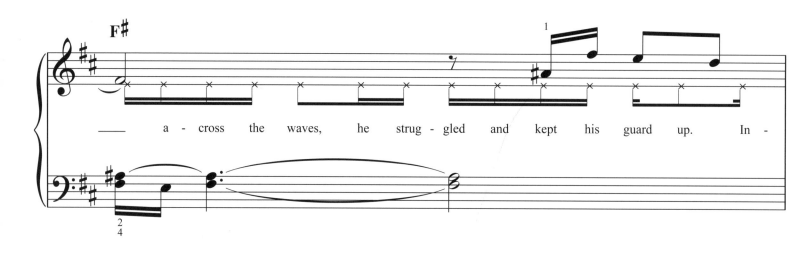

they placed him in charge of a trad-ing char-ter. And ev-'ry day while slaves were be-ing slaugh-tered and cart-ed a-way

F♯

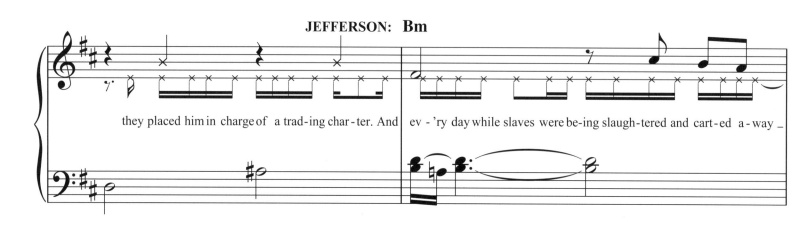

a-cross the waves, he strug-gled and kept his guard up. In-

G   **D**   **F♯7/A♯**   **MADISON:**

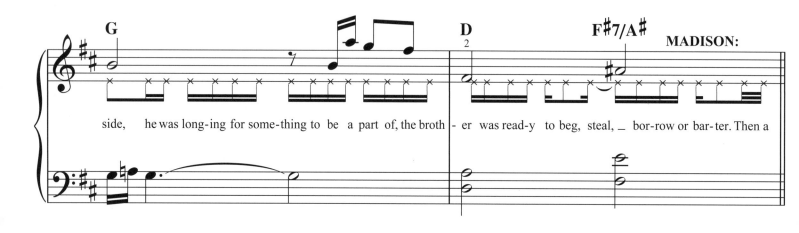

side, he was long-ing for some-thing to be a part of, the broth-er was read-y to beg, steal, bor-row or bar-ter. Then a

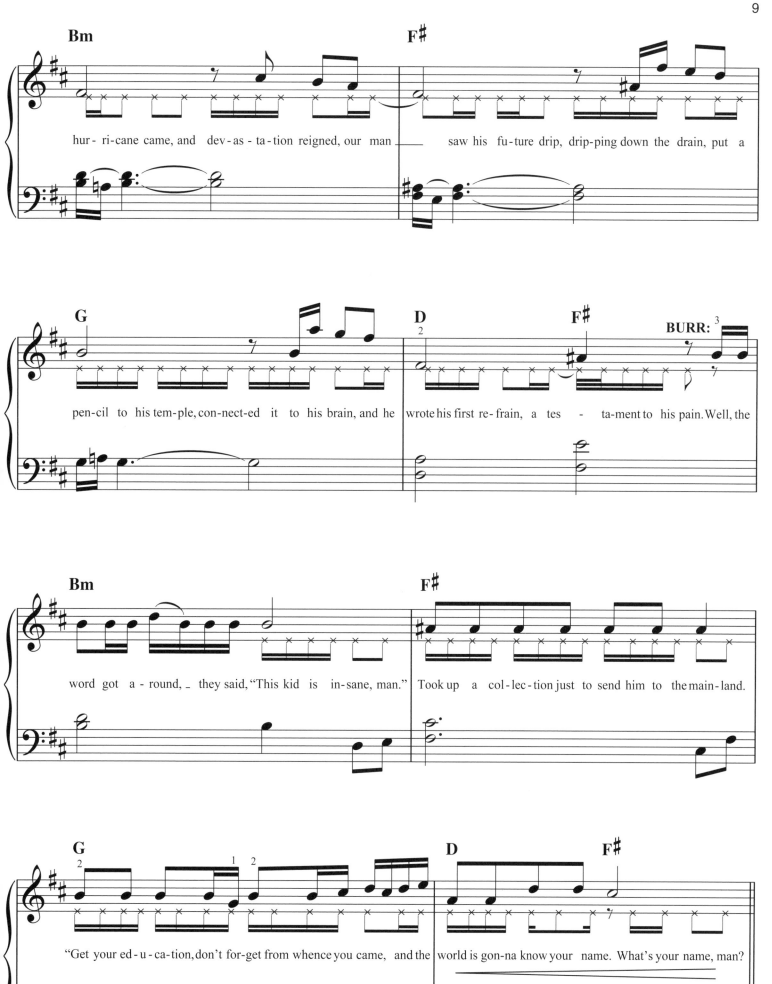

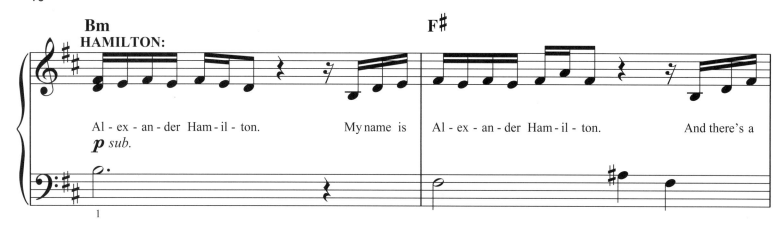

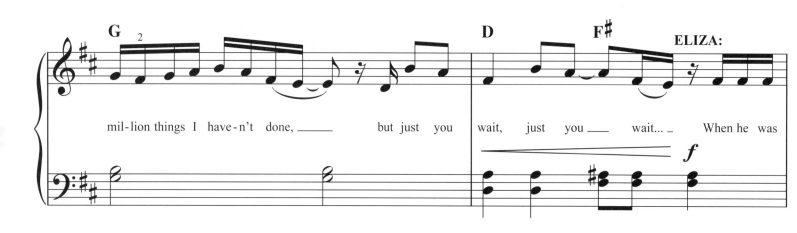

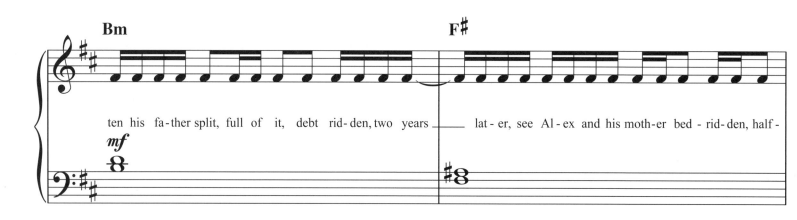

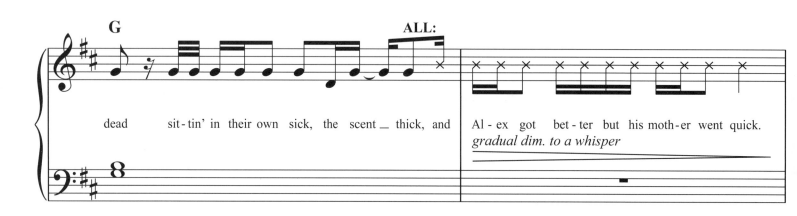

Bm
WASHINGTON:
F#

Moved in with a cous-in, the cous-in com-mit-ted su - i-cide. Left him with noth-in' but ru-ined pride, some-thing new in-side, a

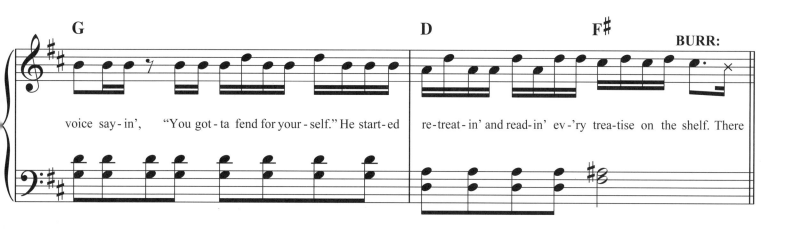

G
D
F#
BURR:

voice say-in', "You got-ta fend for your-self." He start-ed re-treat-in' and read-in' ev-'ry trea-tise on the shelf. There

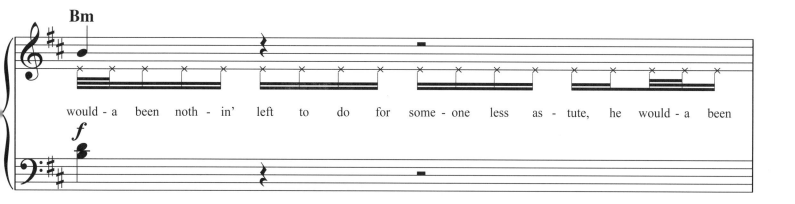

Bm

would-a been noth-in' left to do for some-one less as-tute, he would-a been

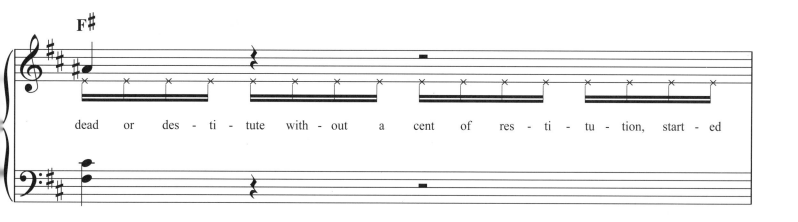

F#

dead or des-ti-tute with-out a cent of res-ti-tu-tion, start-ed

12

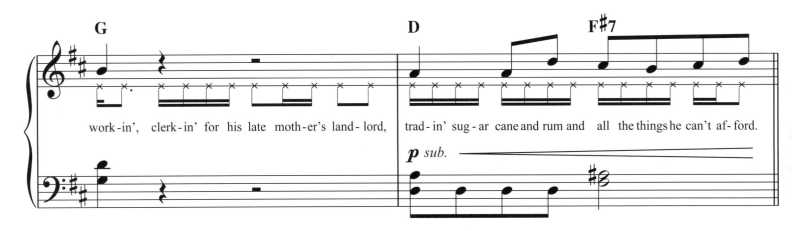

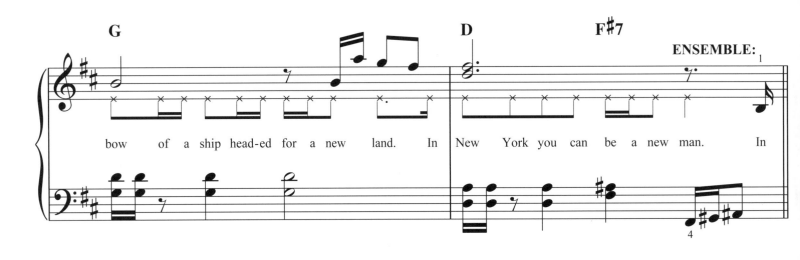

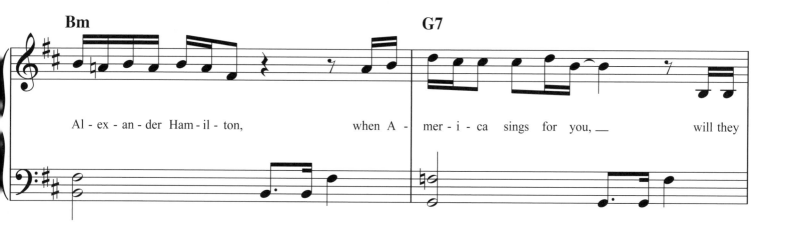

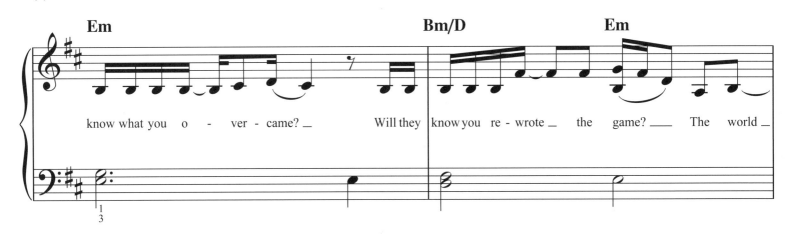

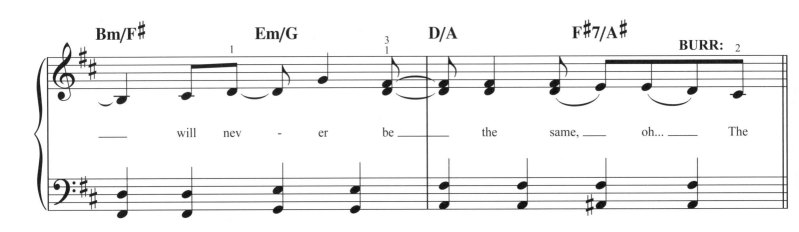

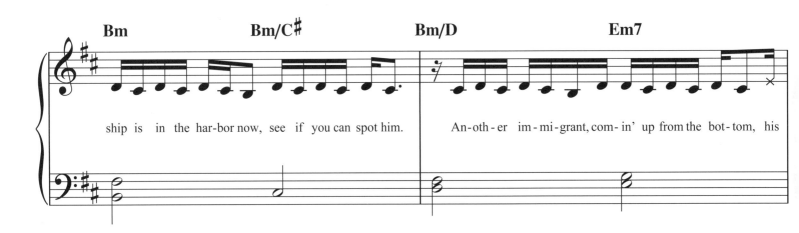

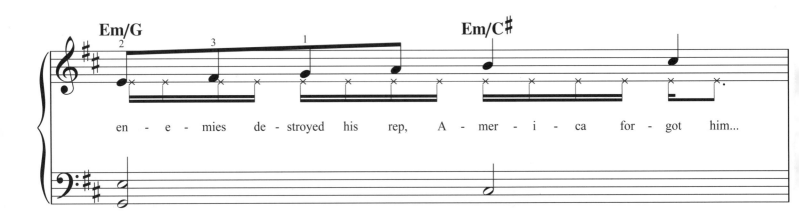

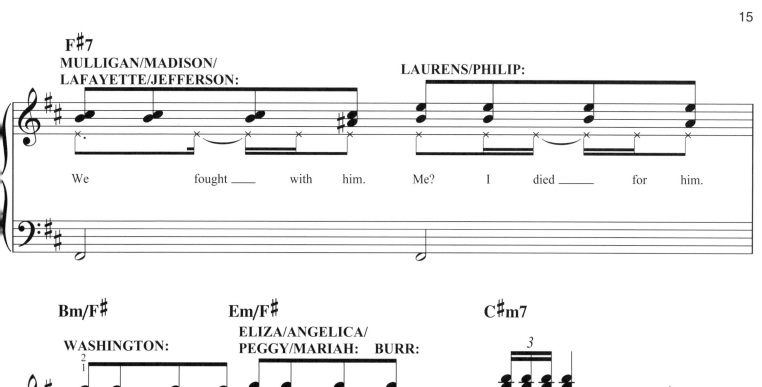

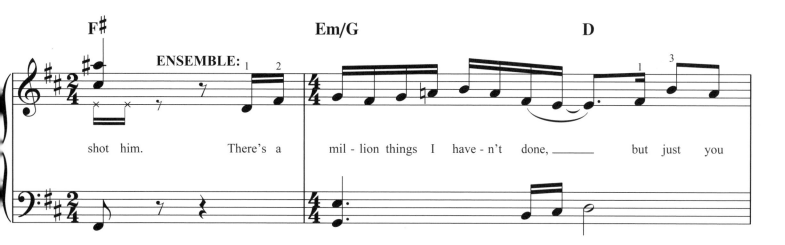

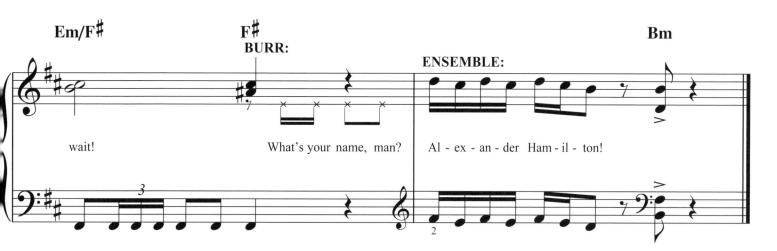

MY SHOT

Words and Music by
LIN-MANUEL MIRANDA
with ALBERT JOHNSON, KEJUAN WALIEK MUCHITA,
OSTEN HARVEY, JR., ROGER TROUTMAN,
CHRISTOPHER WALLACE

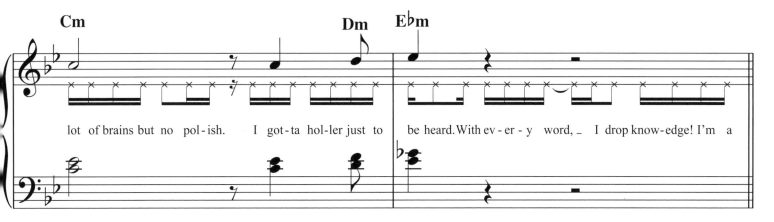

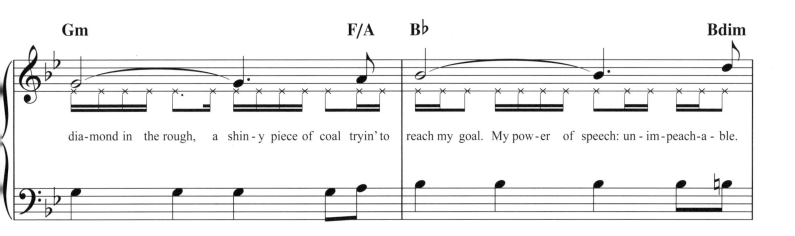

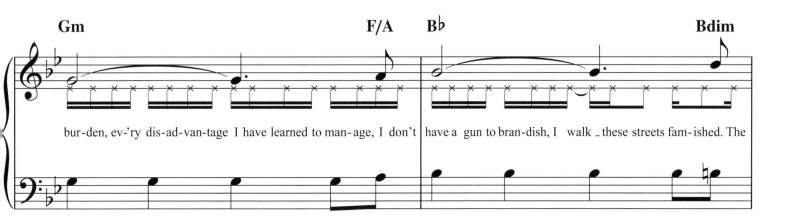

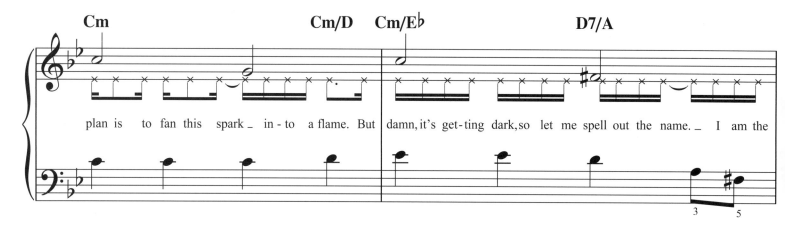

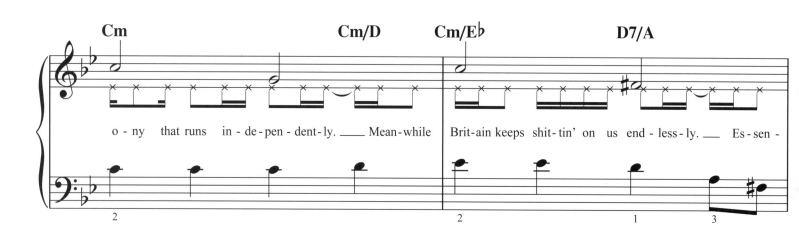

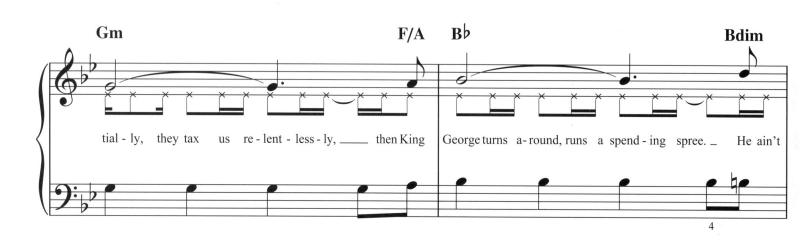

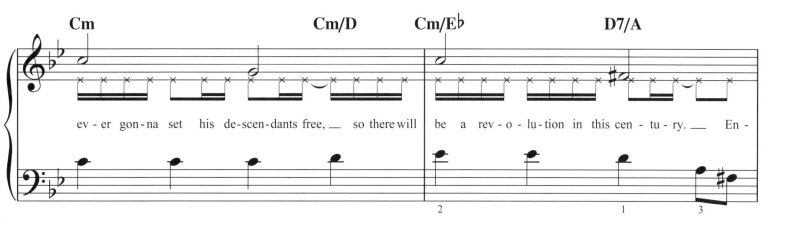

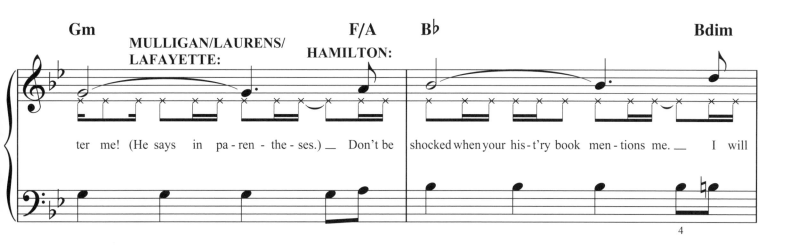

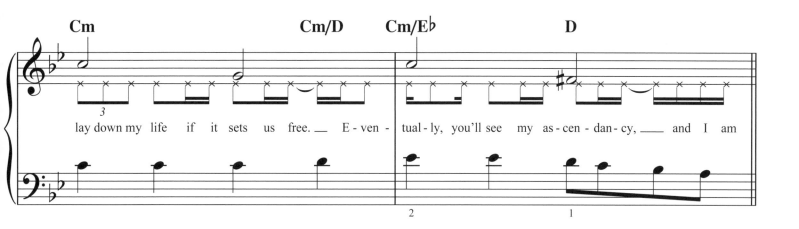

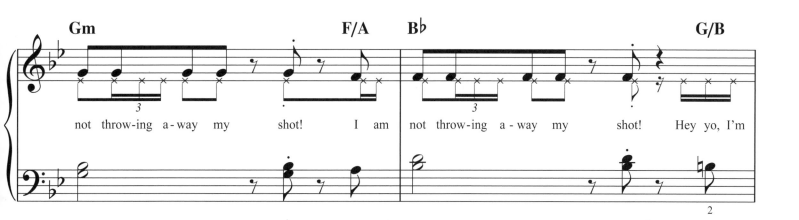

20

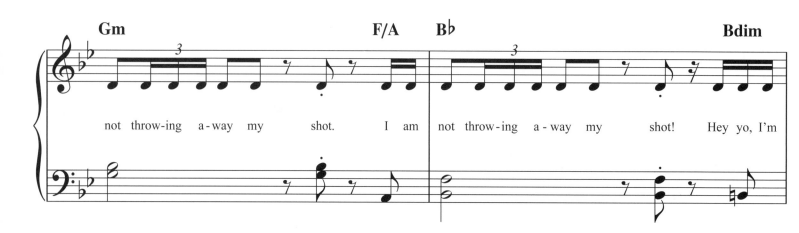

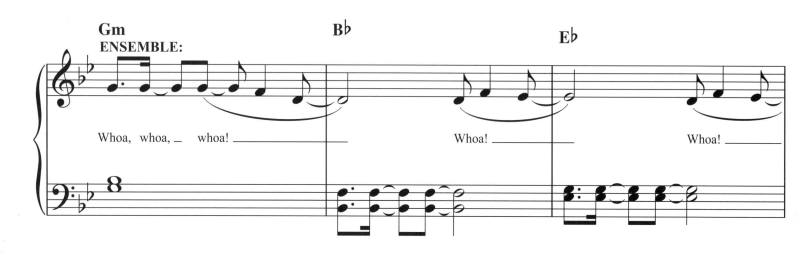

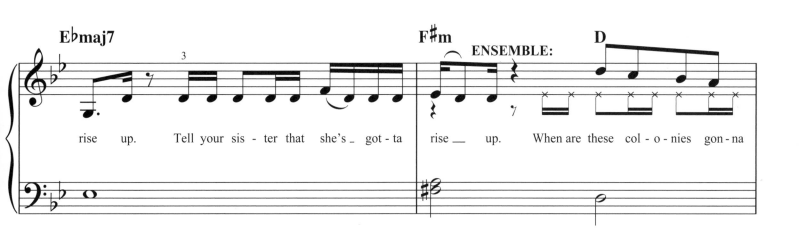

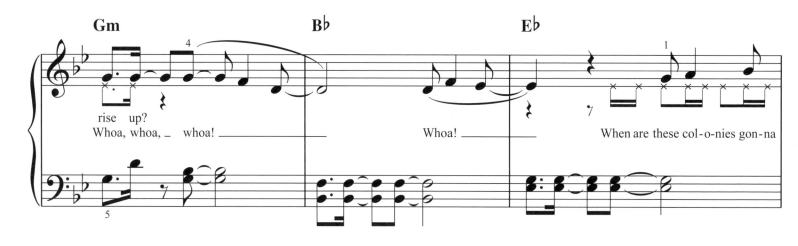

Gm

B♭

E♭

rise up?
Whoa, whoa, _ whoa! _____ Whoa! _____ When are these col-o-nies gon-na

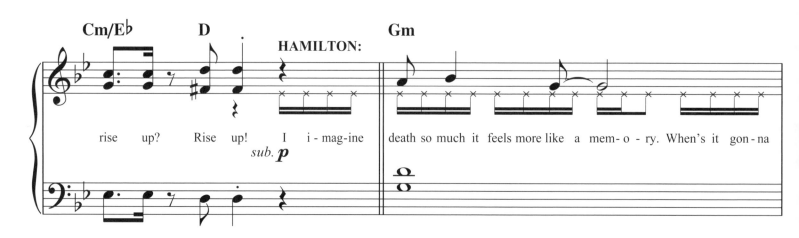

Cm/E♭

D

HAMILTON:

Gm

rise up? Rise up! I i-mag-ine death so much it feels more like a mem-o-ry. When's it gon-na

sub. **p**

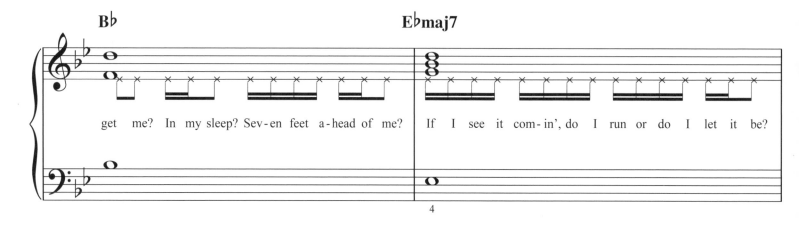

B♭

E♭maj7

get me? In my sleep? Sev-en feet a-head of me? If I see it com-in', do I run or do I let it be?

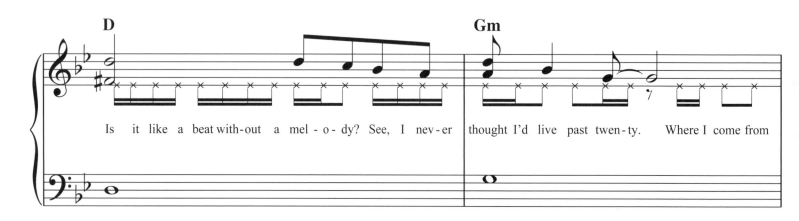

D

Gm

Is it like a beat with-out a mel-o-dy? See, I nev-er thought I'd live past twen-ty. Where I come from

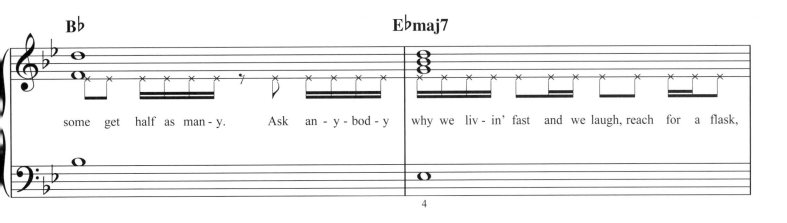

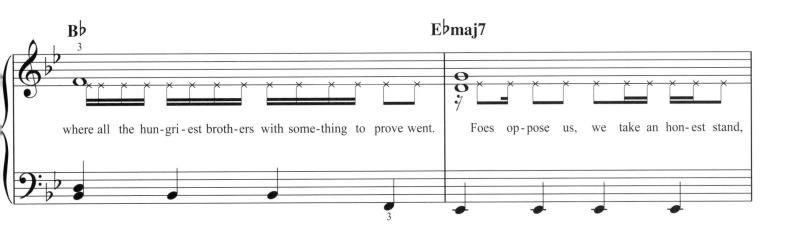

24

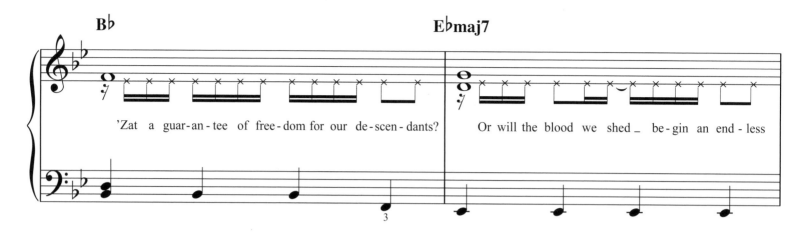

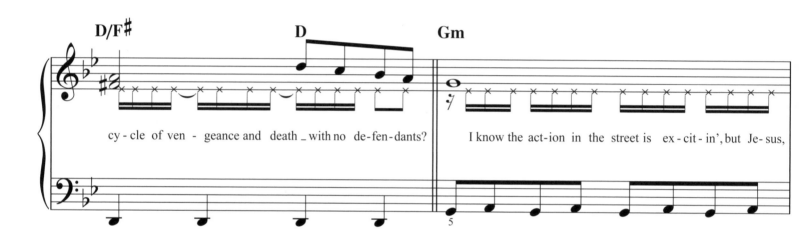

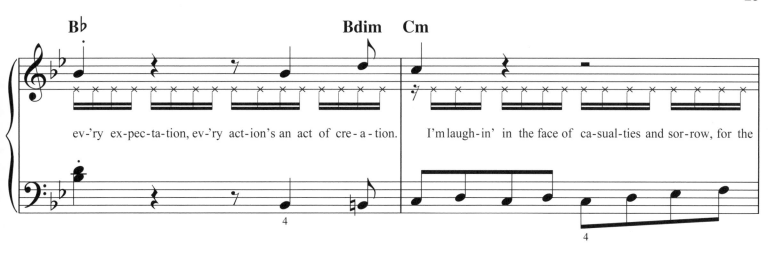

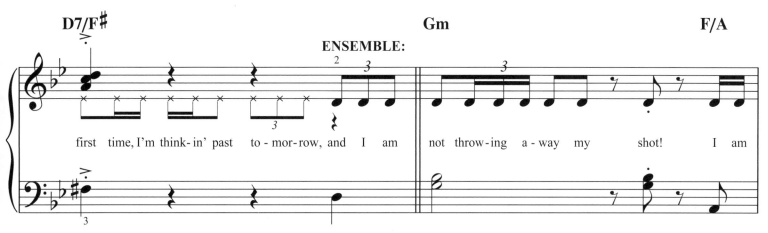

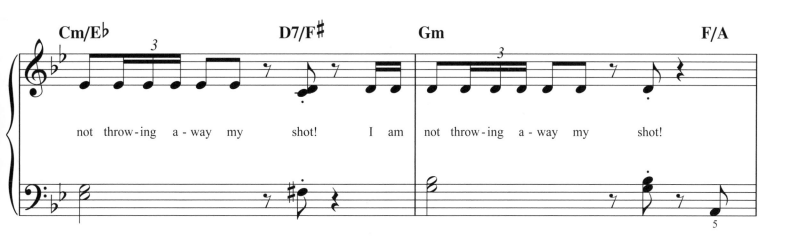

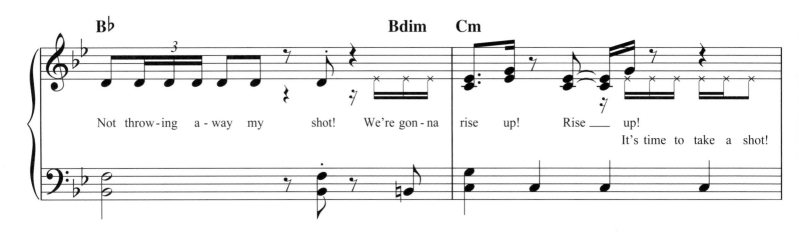

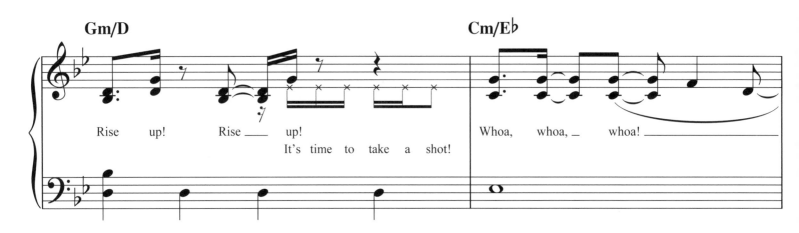

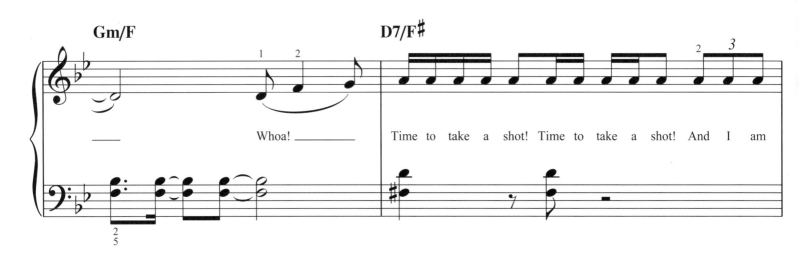

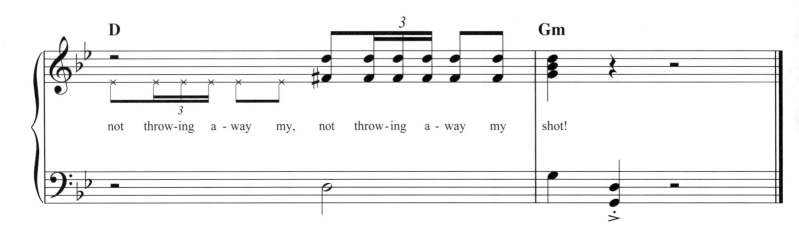

THE SCHUYLER SISTERS

Words and Music by
LIN-MANUEL MIRANDA

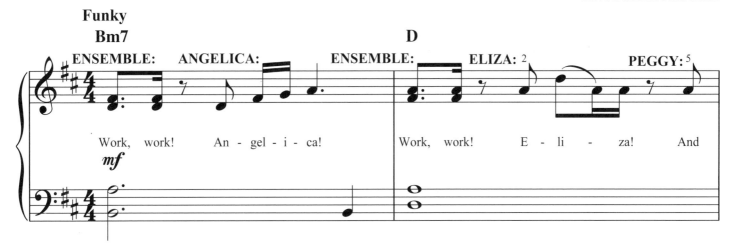

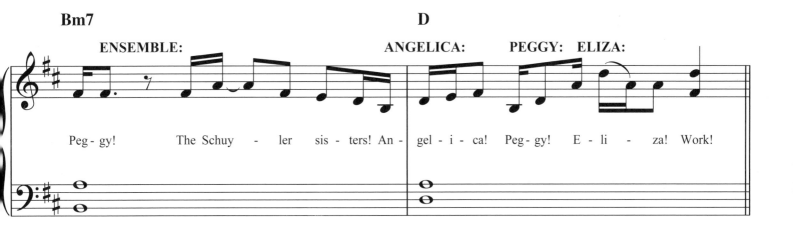

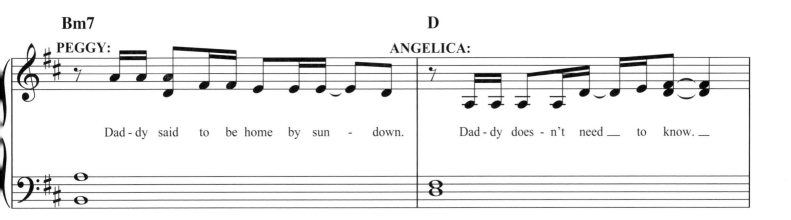

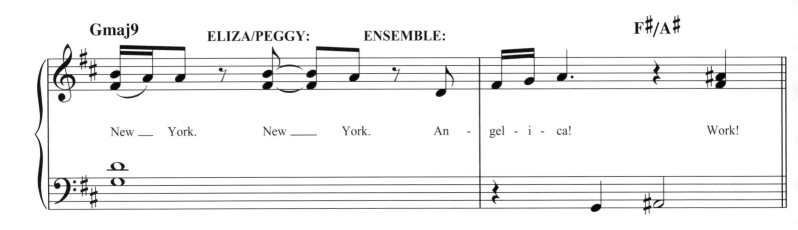

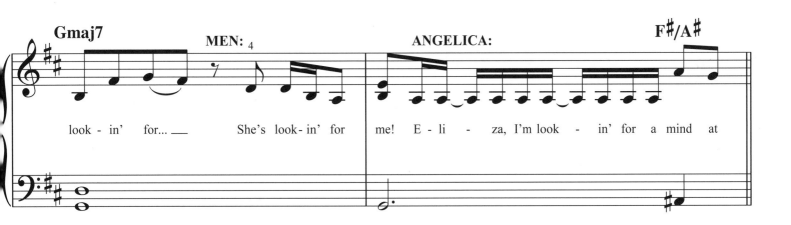

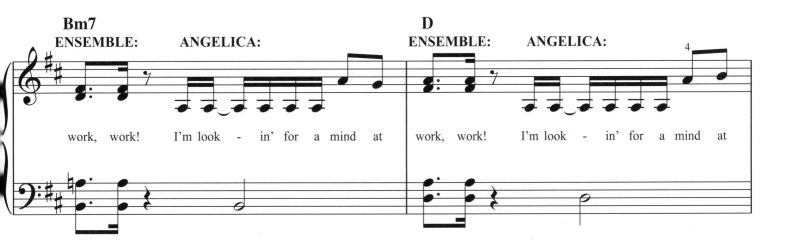

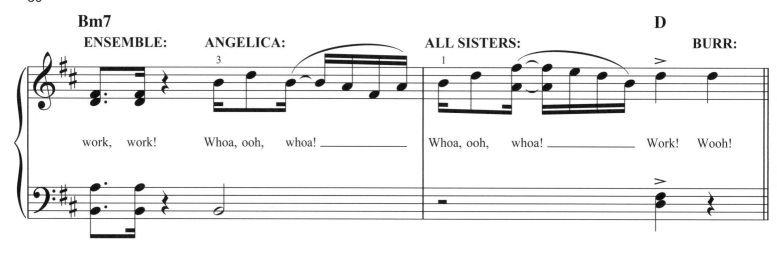

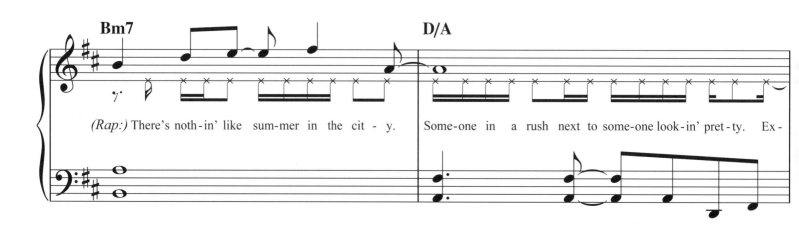

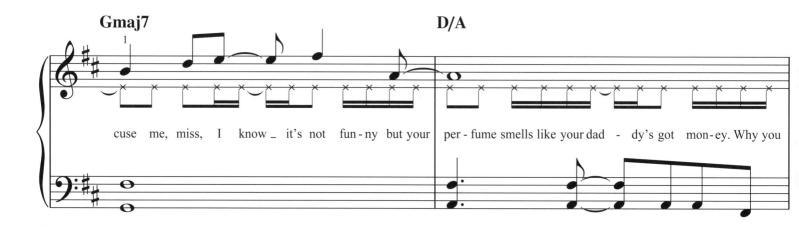

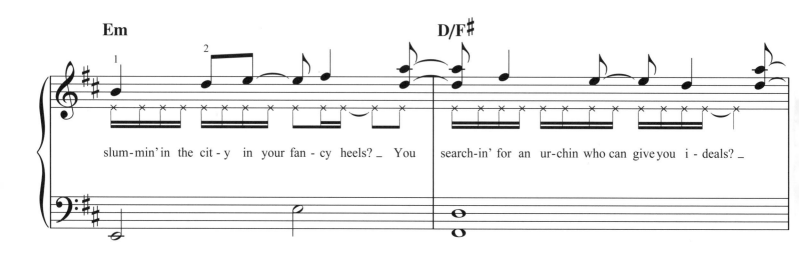

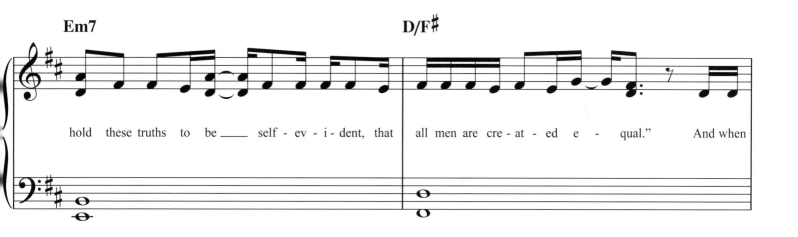

Gmaj9   **F#7/A#**

I meet Thom-as Jef-fer-son, I'm-'a com-pel him to in- clude *wom-en* in the se - quel! Work!

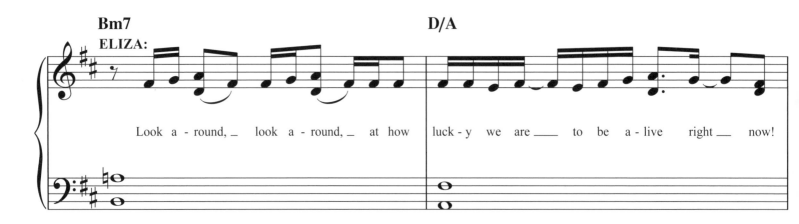

Bm7   **D/A**

ELIZA:

Look a - round, _ look a - round, _ at how luck-y we are ___ to be a-live right ___ now!

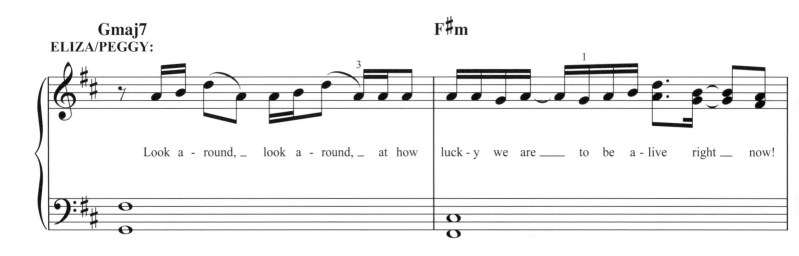

Gmaj7   **F#m**

ELIZA/PEGGY:

Look a - round, _ look a - round, _ at how luck-y we are ___ to be a-live right ___ now!

Em9   **D/F#**

ALL SISTERS:

His - to-ry is hap - pen-in' in Man- hat-an and we ___ just hap - pen to be ___ in the

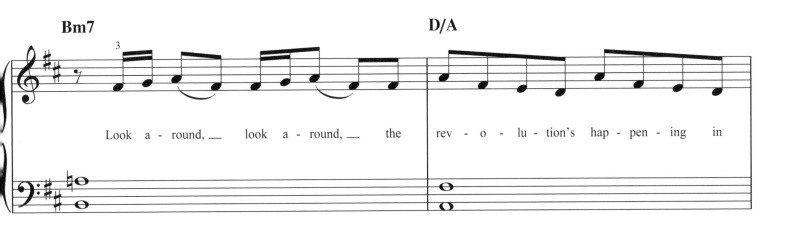

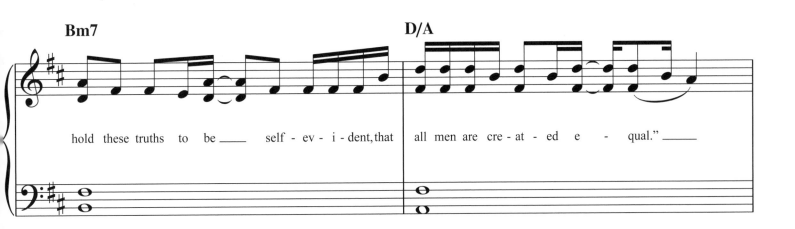

34

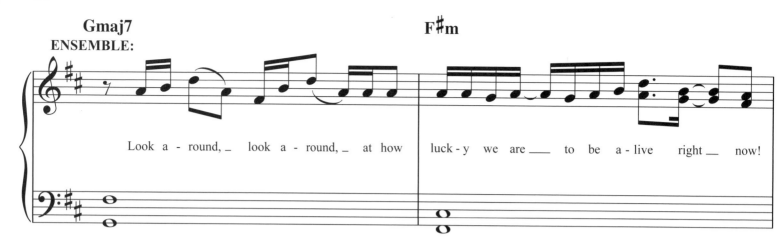

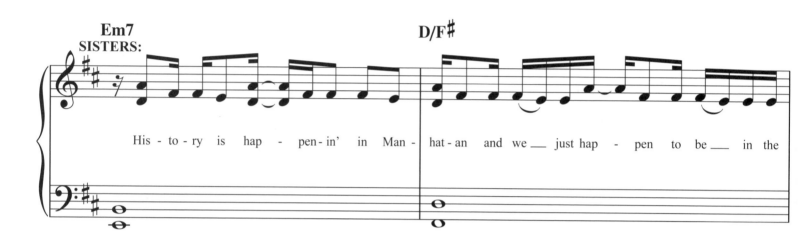

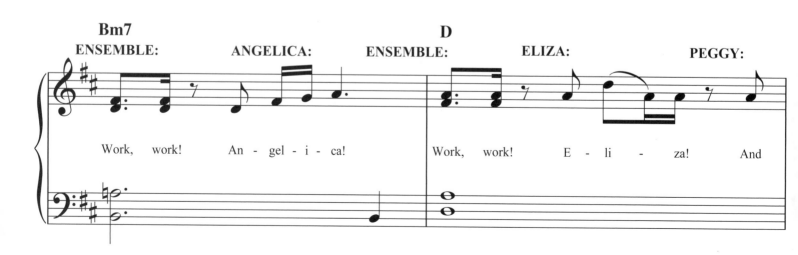

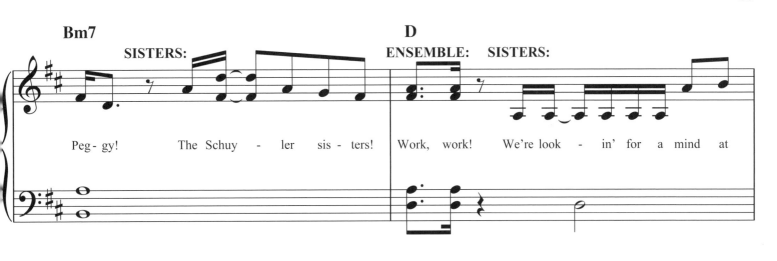

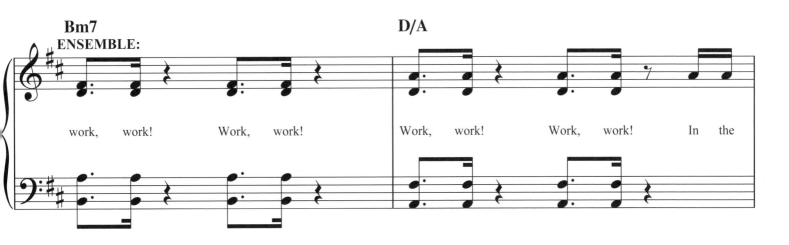

YOU'LL BE BACK

Words and Music by
LIN-MANUEL MIRANDA

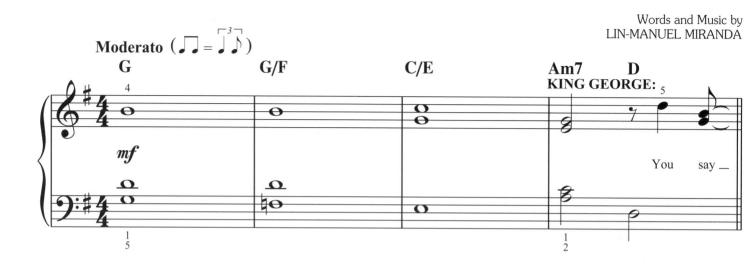

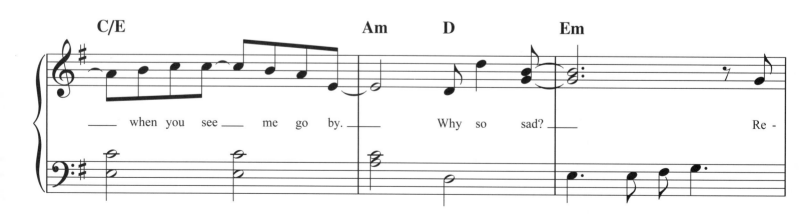

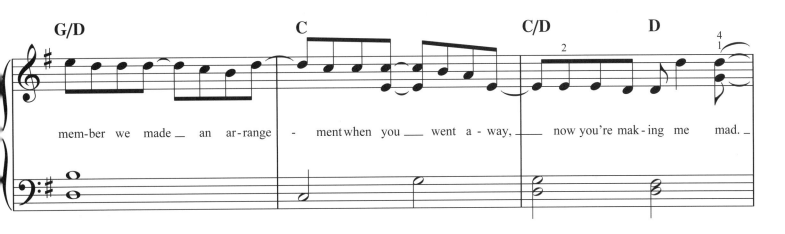

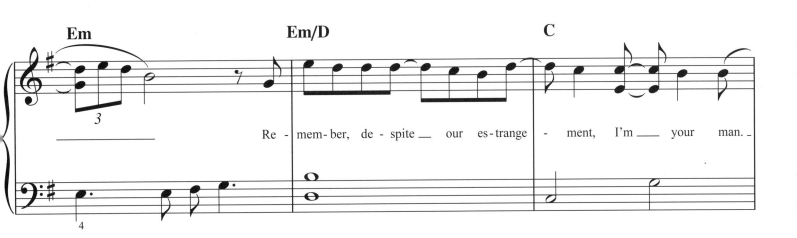

38

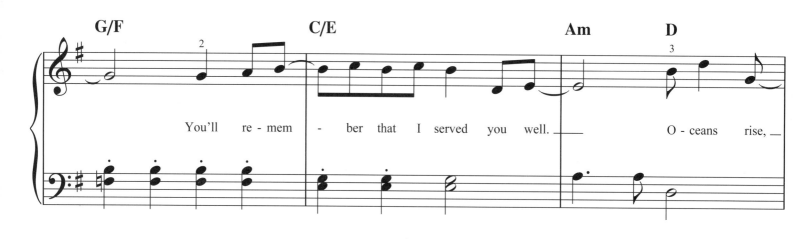

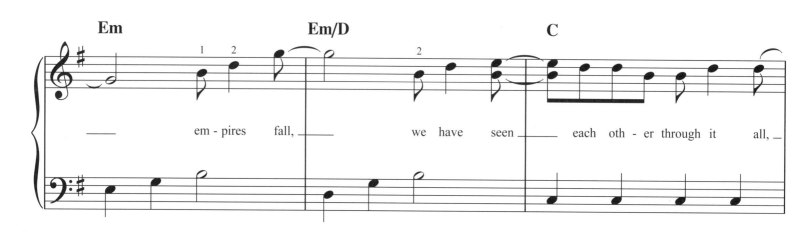

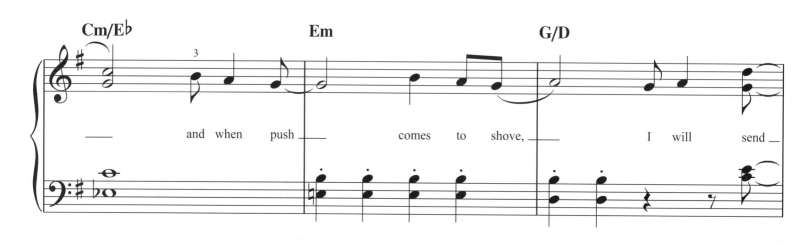

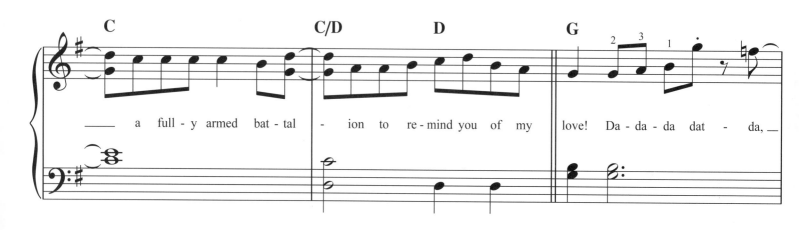

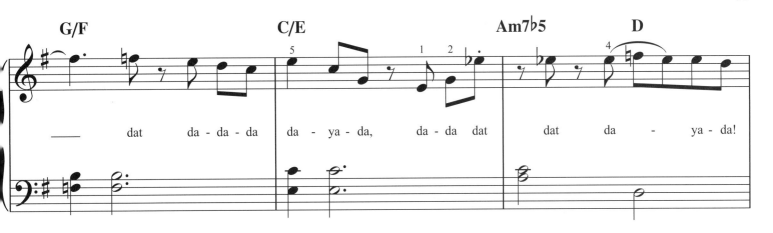

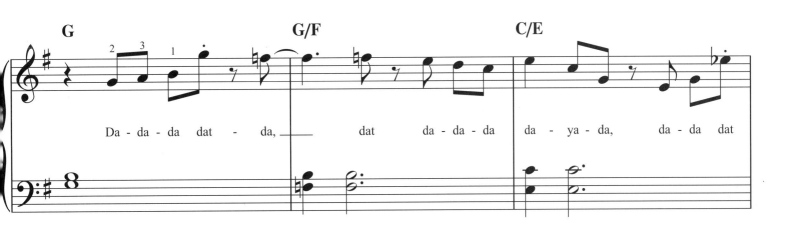

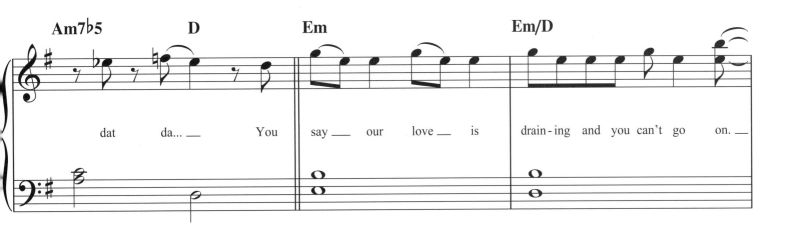

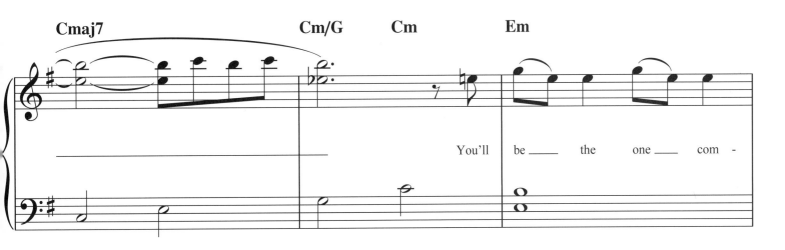

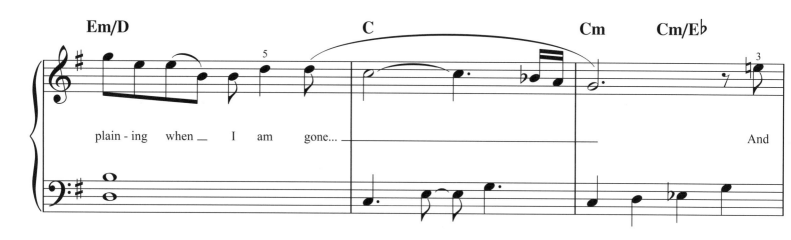

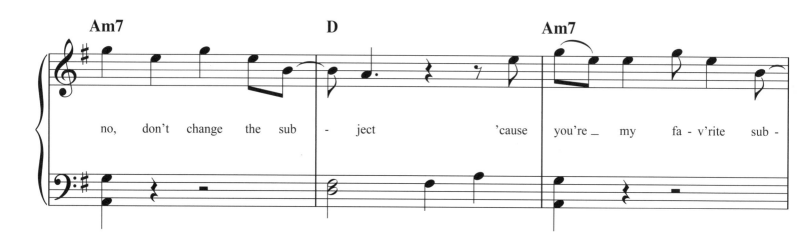

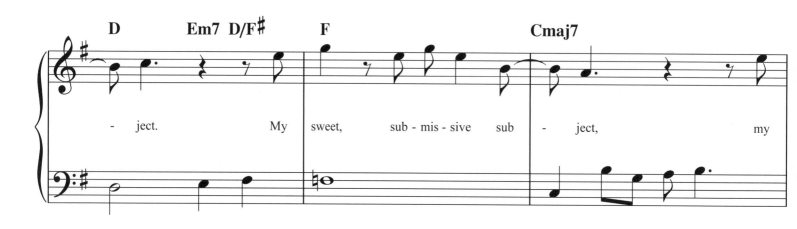

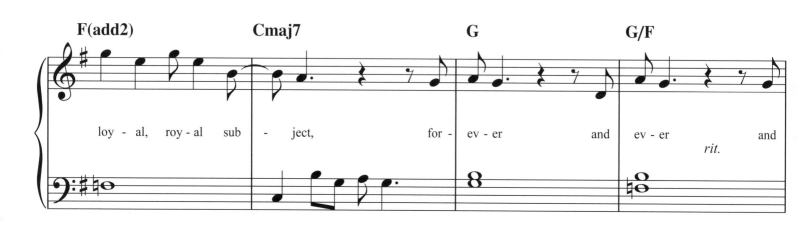

42

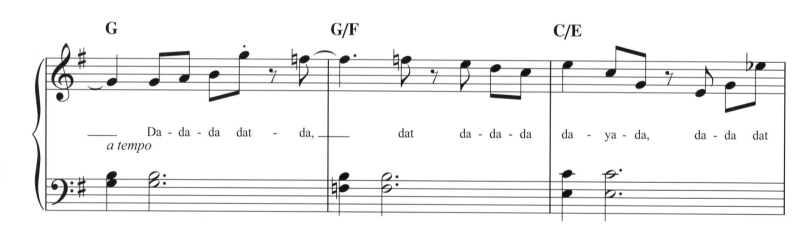

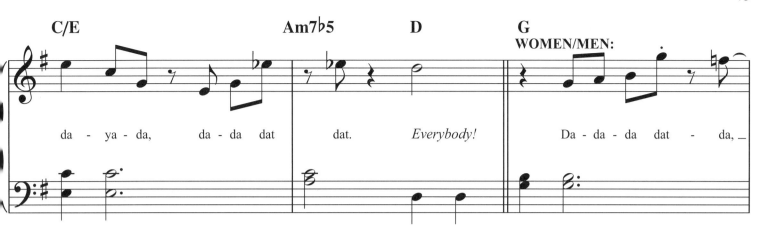

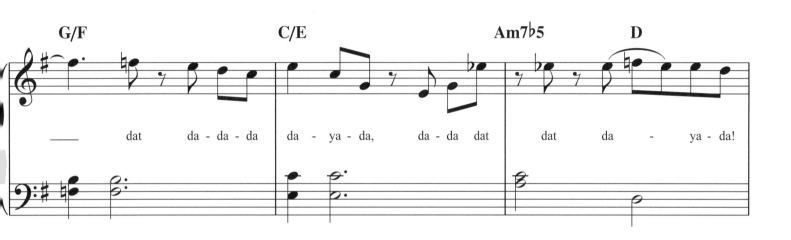

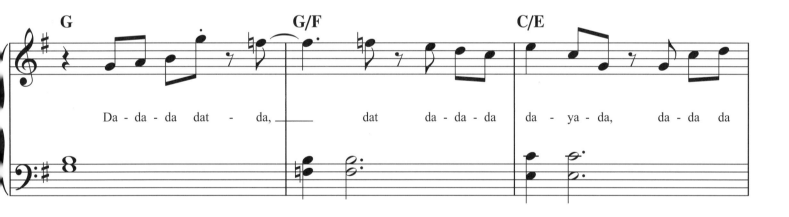

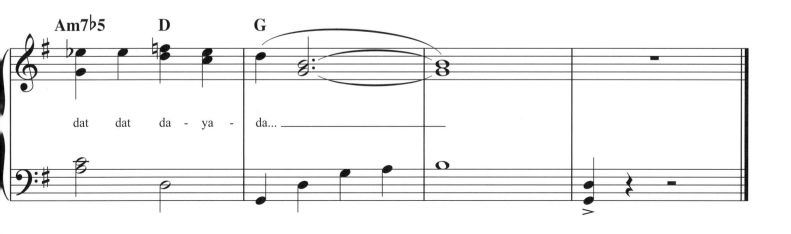

HELPLESS

Words and Music by
LIN-MANUEL MIRANDA

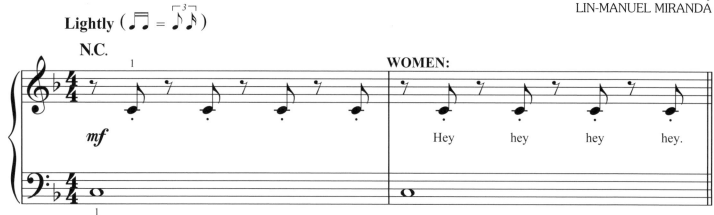

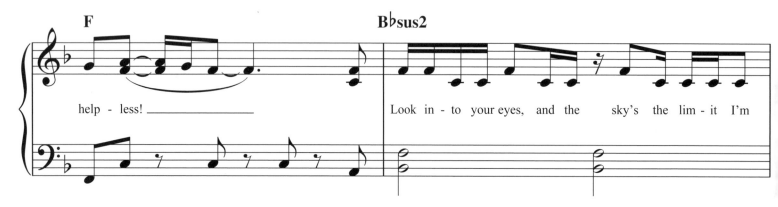

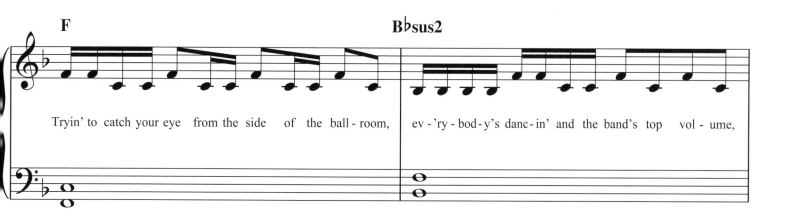

Grind to the rhy-thm as we wine and dine. Grab my sis - ter, and whis - per, "Yo, this one's mine."

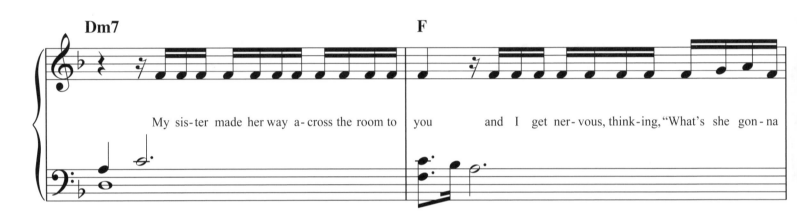

My sis-ter made her way a-cross the room to you and I get ner-vous, think-ing, "What's she gon-na

do?" She grabs you by the arm, I'm think-in', "I'm through." Then you look back at me and sud-den-ly I'm

help - less! Oh, look at those eyes. Oh! Yeah, I'm

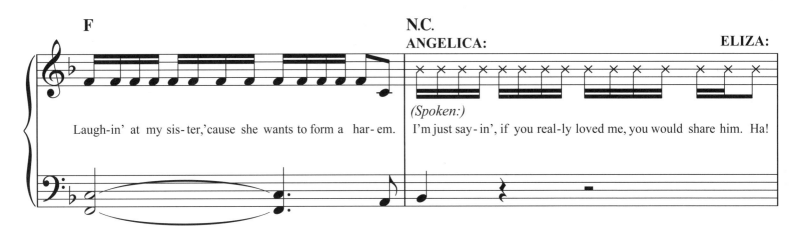

Laugh-in' at my sis-ter,'cause she wants to form a har-em.

ANGELICA: I'm just say-in', if you real-ly loved me, you would share him. Ha!

(Spoken:)

Two weeks lat-er, in the liv-ing room, stress-in', my fa-ther's stone-faced while you're ask-ing for his bless-in'. I'm

dy-ing in-side, as you wine and dine ___ and I'm tryin' not to cry,'cause there's noth-ing that your mind can't

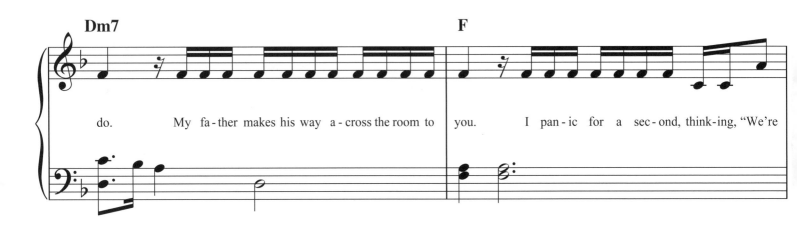

do. My fa-ther makes his way a-cross the room to you. I pan-ic for a sec-ond, think-ing, "We're

B♭sus2

Csus

through." _____ But then he shakes your hand and says, "Be true." _____ And you turn back to me, smil-ing, and I...

F

B♭sus2

WOMEN:

Help - less! _____ Look in - to your eyes, and the sky's the lim - it I'm

F

1.

B♭sus2

help - less! _____ Down for the count, and I'm drown - in' in 'em.

2.

B♭sus2

ELIZA:

HAMILTON:

N.C.

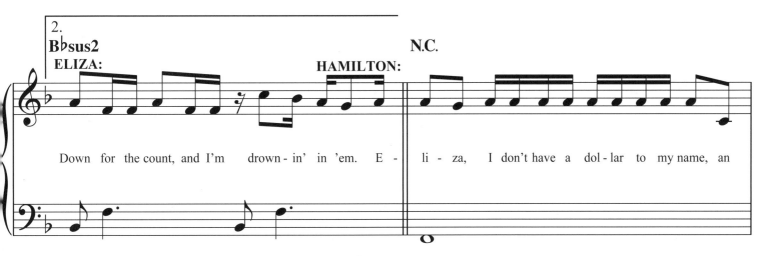

Down for the count, and I'm drown - in' in 'em. E - li - za, I don't have a dol - lar to my name, an

a-cre of land, a troop to com-mand, a dol-lop of fame. All I have's my hon-or, a tol-er-ance for pain, a cou-

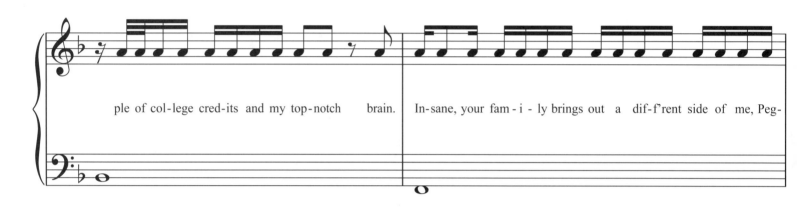

ple of col-lege cred-its and my top-notch brain. In-sane, your fam-i-ly brings out a dif-f'rent side of me, Peg-

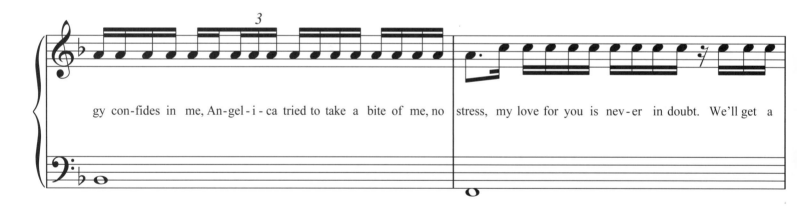

gy con-fides in me, An-gel-i-ca tried to take a bite of me, no stress, my love for you is nev-er in doubt. We'll get a

Dm7

lit-tle place in Har-lem and we'll fig-ure it out. I've been liv- in'with-out a fam-i-ly since I was a child. _ My fa-ther

F　　　　　　　　　　　　　　**B♭sus2**

left, my moth-er died, I grew up buck wild. __ But I'll __ nev-er for get my moth-er's face, that was real, __ and long as

C7　　　　　　　　　　　　　　**F**　WOMEN:

I'm a - live, E - li - za, swear to God, you'll nev - er feel __ so... help - less! _____

B♭　　　　　　　　　　　　　　**F**
ELIZA:　　　　　　　　　　　　　WOMEN:

I do, I do, I do, I dooo! _____ Help - less! _____

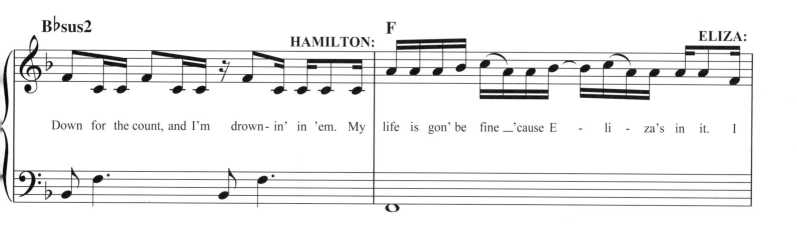

B♭sus2　　　　　　　　　　　　**F**
　　　　　　　　HAMILTON:　　　　　　　　　　　　　ELIZA:

Down for the count, and I'm drown- in' in 'em. My life is gon' be fine __ 'cause E - li - za's in it. I

look in - to your eyes, and the sky's the lim - it I'm help - less! _____

Down for the count, and I'm drown - in' in 'em.

WOMEN:

In

New York, __ you can __ be a new man, __ in New York, __ you can __ be a new man, __ in

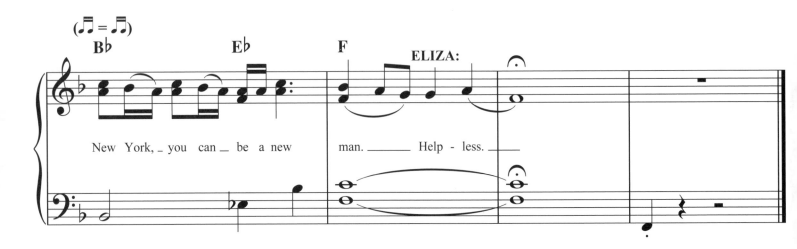

New York, __ you can __ be a new man. ELIZA: Help - less.

WAIT FOR IT

Words and Music by
LIN-MANUEL MIRANDA

Allegro (Feeling of 2)

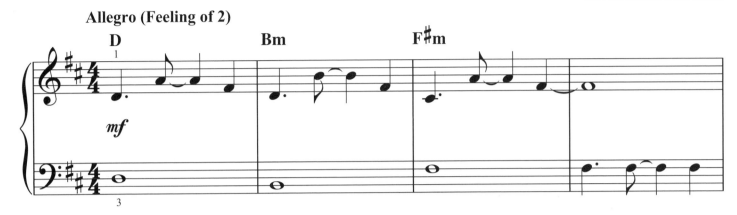

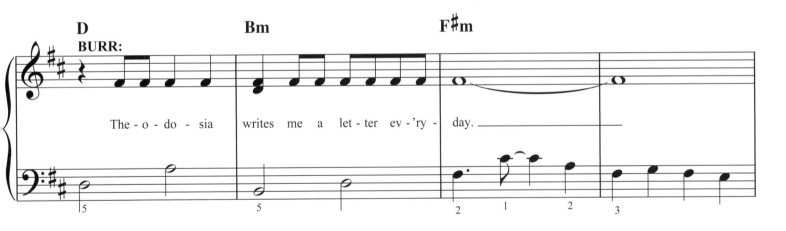

BURR:

The - o - do - sia writes me a let - ter ev - 'ry - day. _____

I'm keep-ing her bed warm while her hus-band is a - way. _____

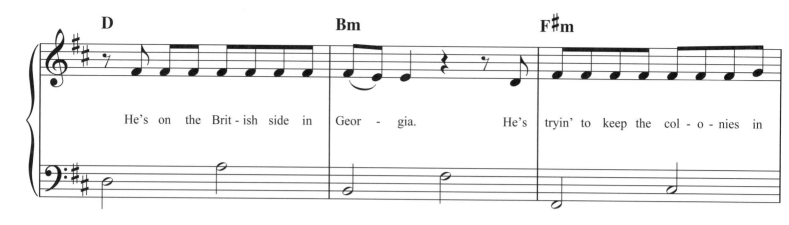

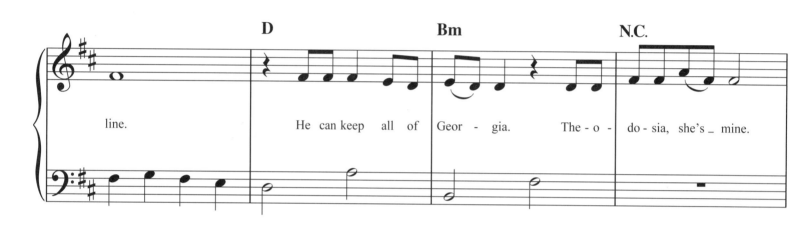

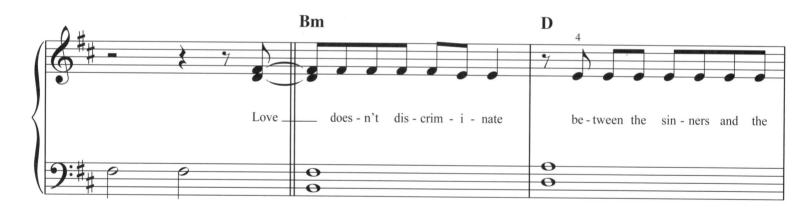

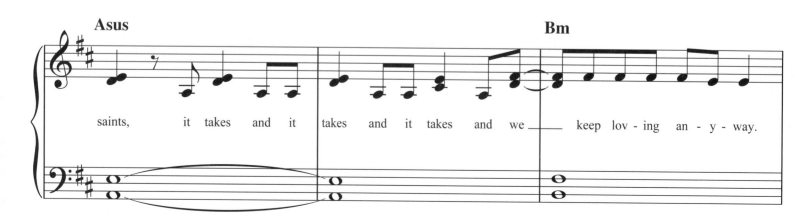

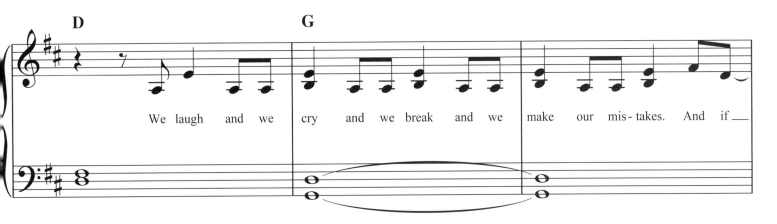

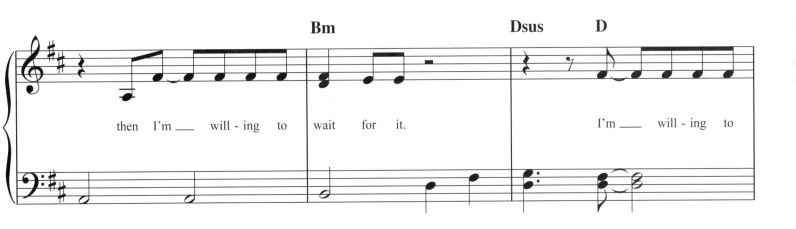

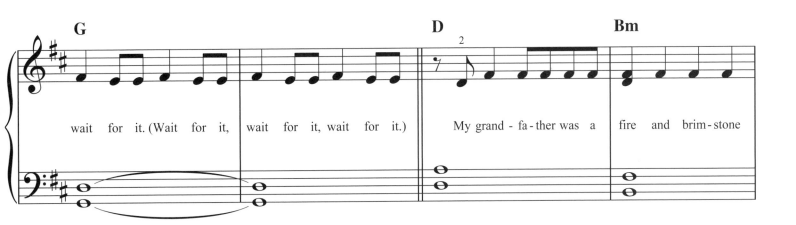

56

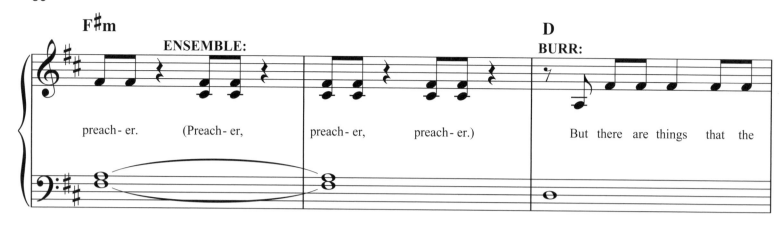

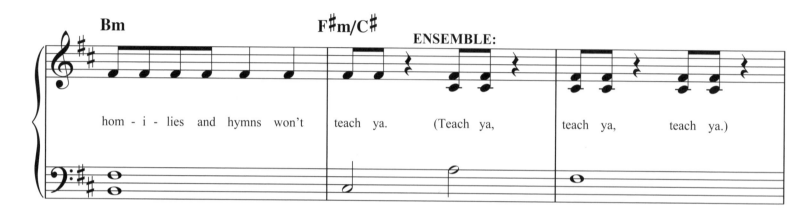

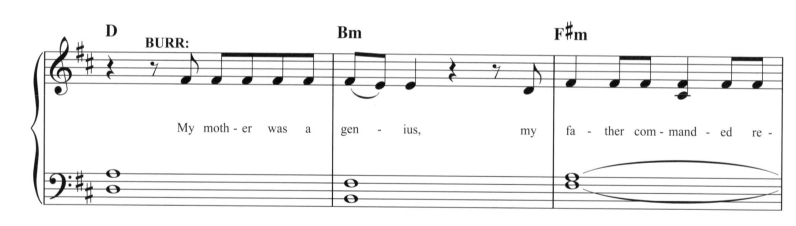

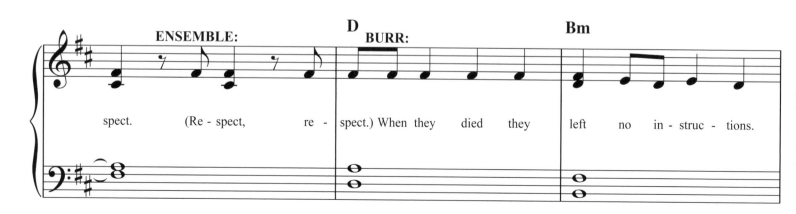

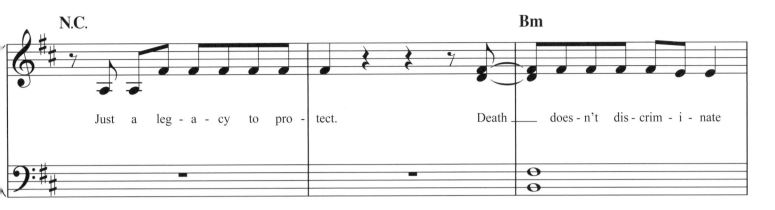

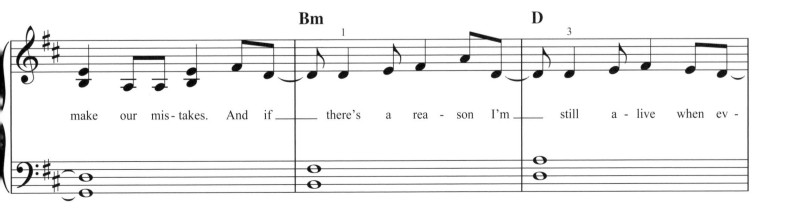

58

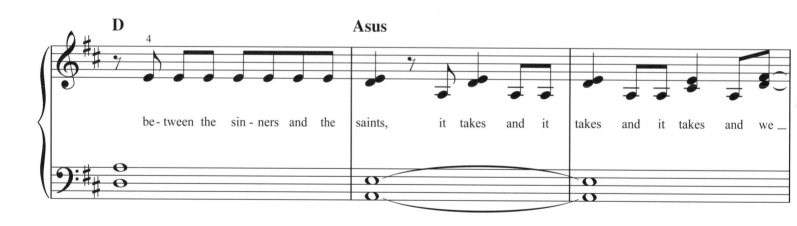

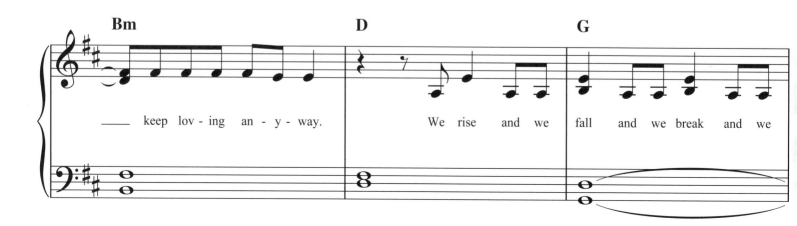

THAT WOULD BE ENOUGH

Words and Music by
LIN-MANUEL MIRANDA

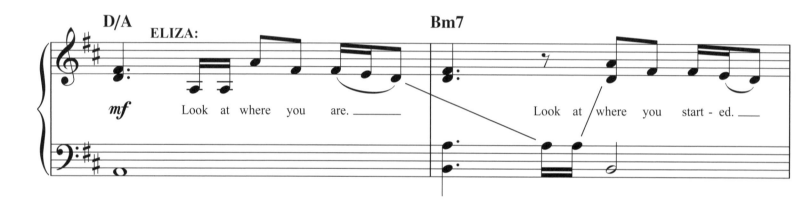

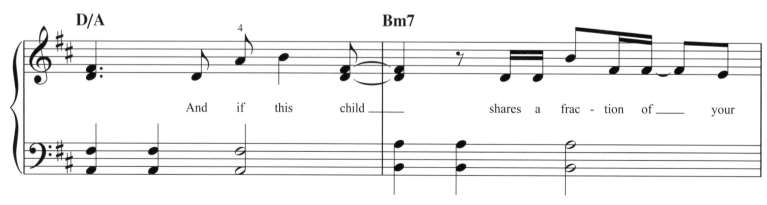

smile __ or a frag - ment of your mind, ___ look out, world! __ That would be e - nough.

I don't pre - tend __ to know ___ the chal - leng - es ___ you're

fac - ing. The worlds you keep __ e - ras - ing and cre - at - ing in your

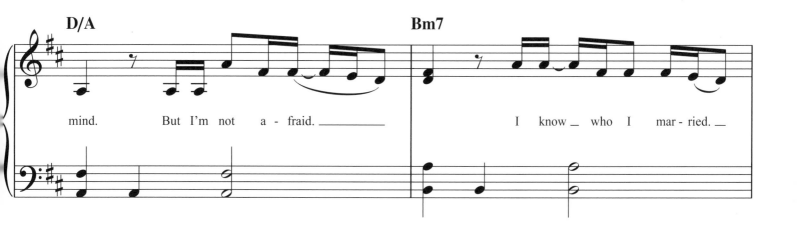

mind. But I'm not a - fraid. ___ I know __ who I mar - ried. __

62

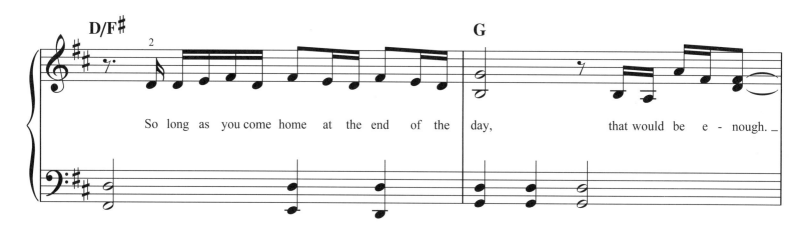

So long as you come home at the end of the day, that would be e - nough. __

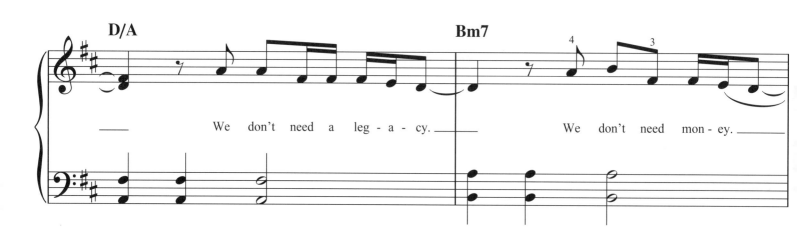

__ We don't need a leg - a - cy. __ We don't need mon - ey. __

__ If I could grant you peace __ of mind, __ if you could let me in - side __ your

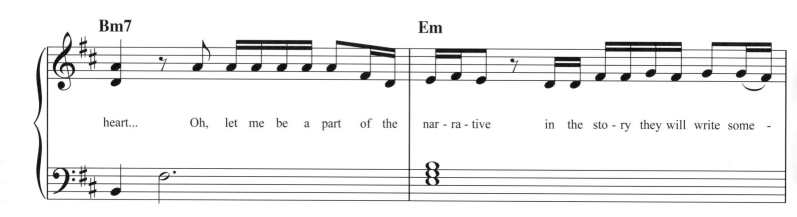

heart... Oh, let me be a part of the nar - ra - tive in the sto - ry they will write some -

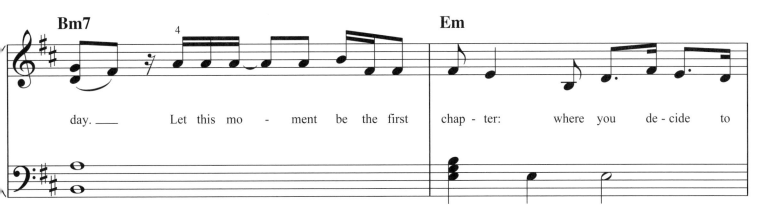

day. _____ Let this mo - ment be the first chap - ter: where you de - cide to

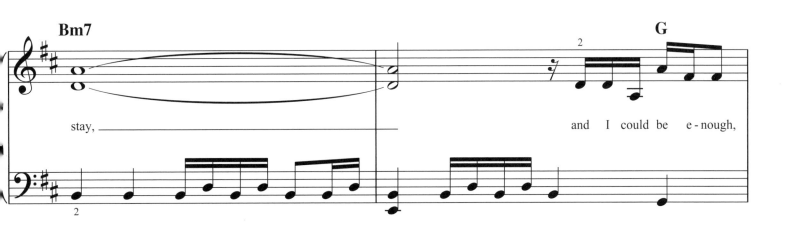

stay, _____ and I could be e - nough,

and we could be e - nough... That would be e - nough. _

rit. _____ a tempo rall.

DEAR THEODOSIA

Words and Music by
LIN-MANUEL MIRANDA

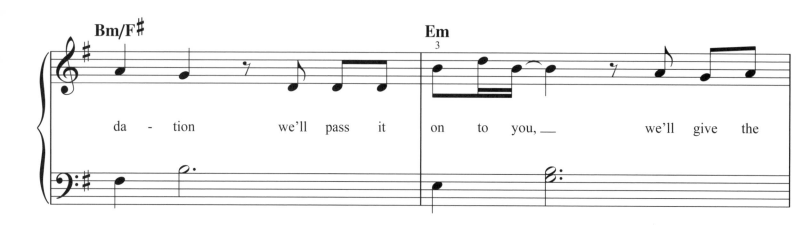

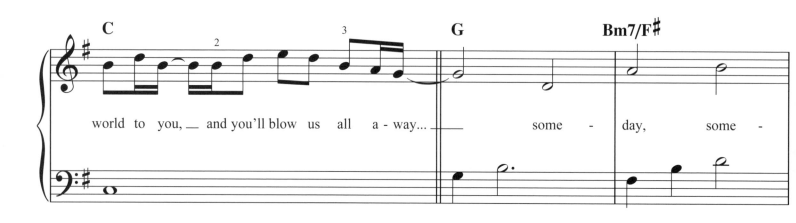

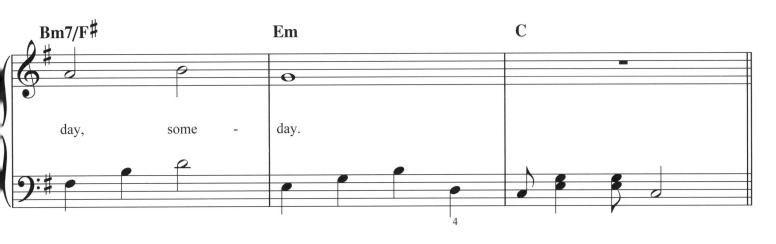

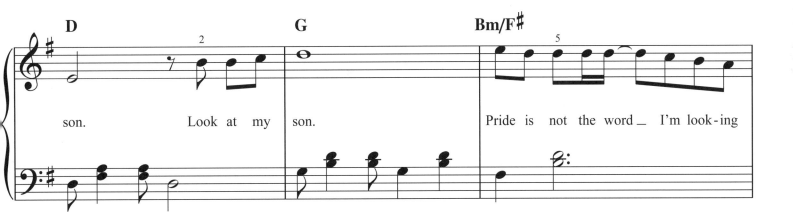

68

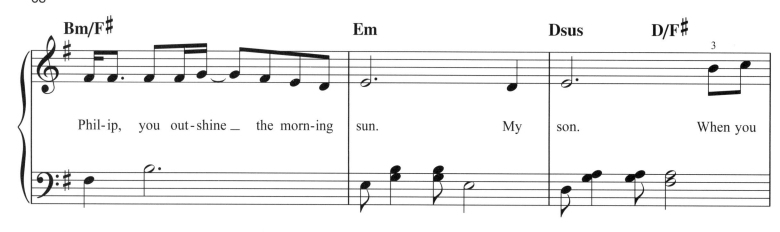

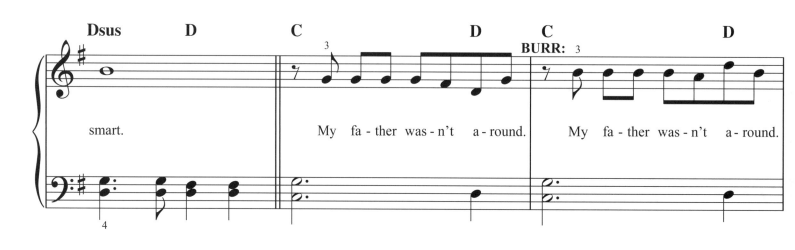

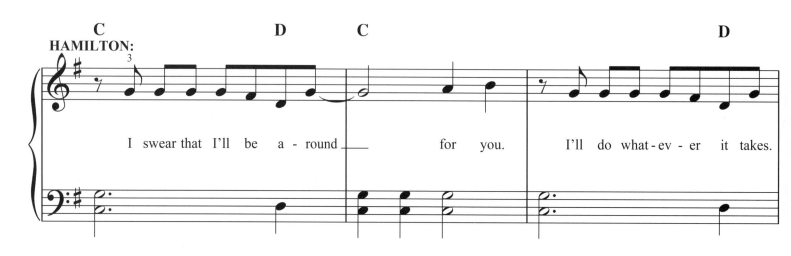

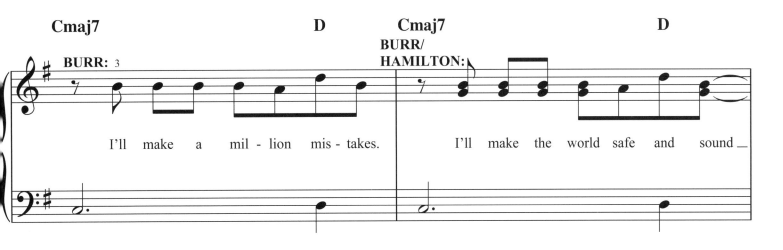

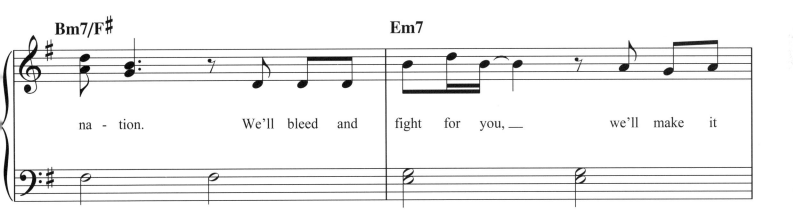

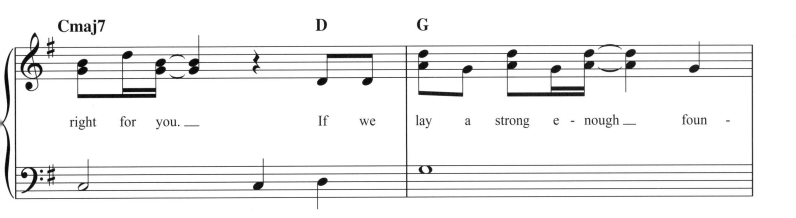

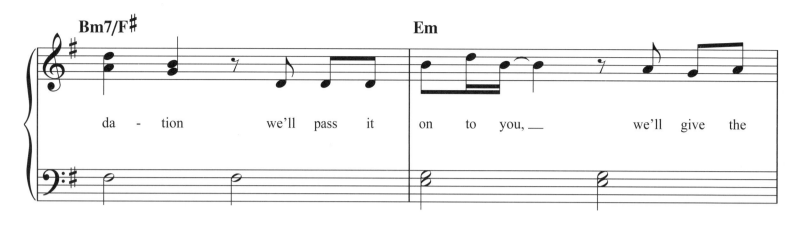

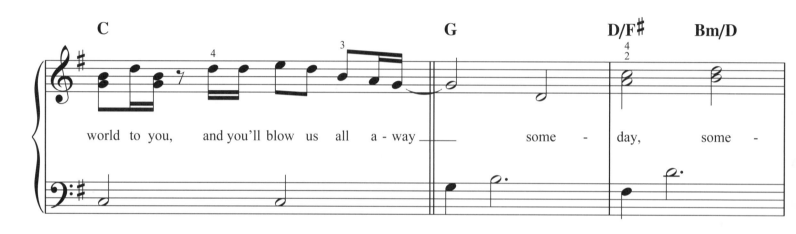

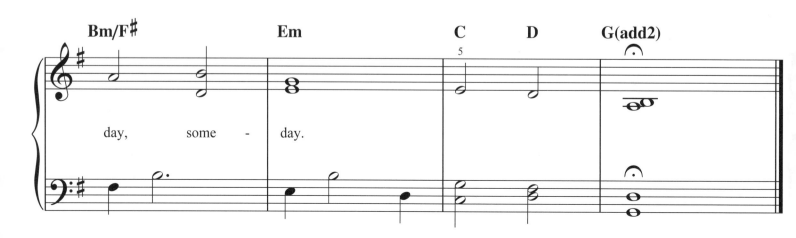

BURN

Words and Music by
LIN-MANUEL MIRANDA

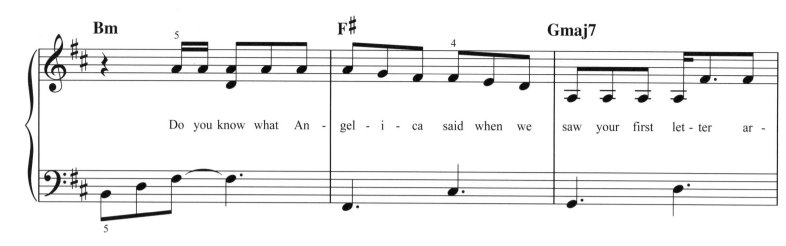

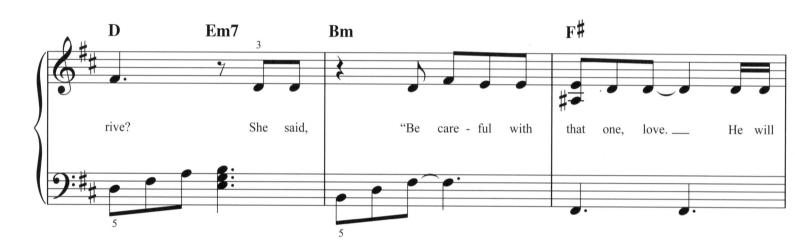

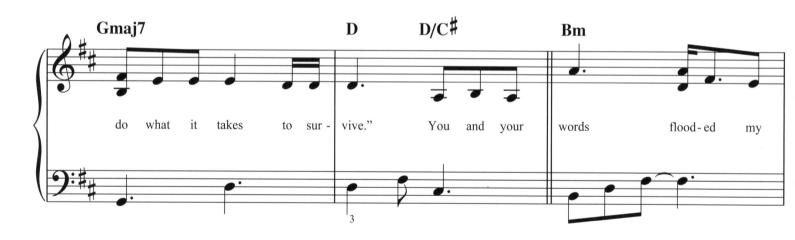

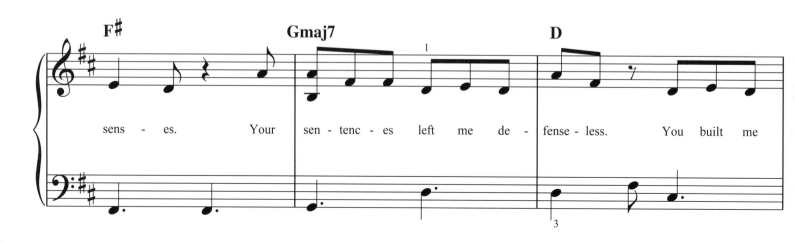

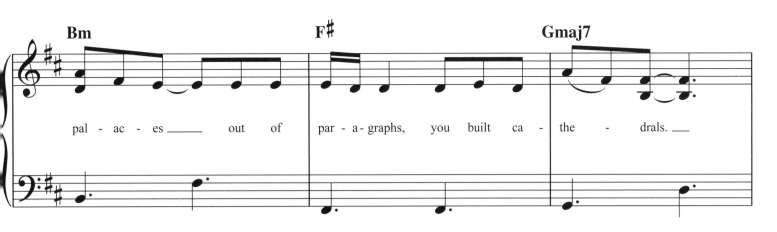

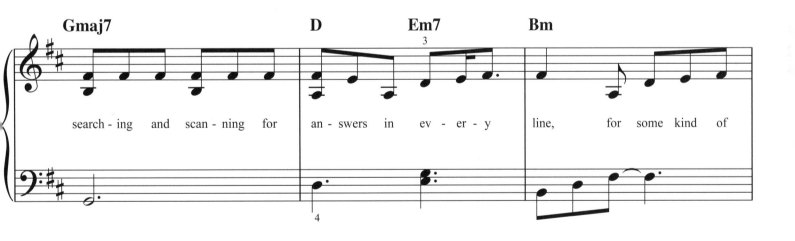

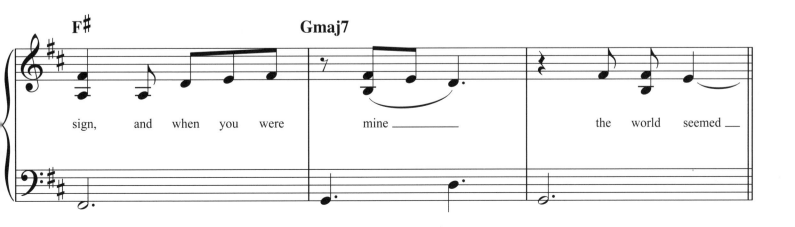

74

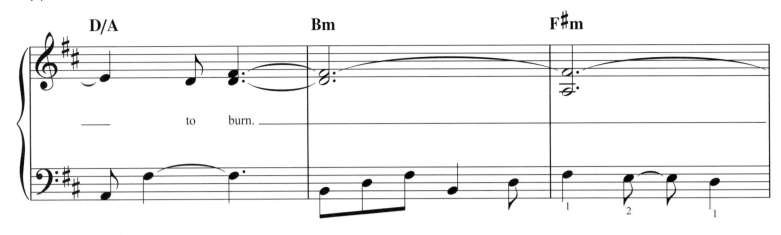

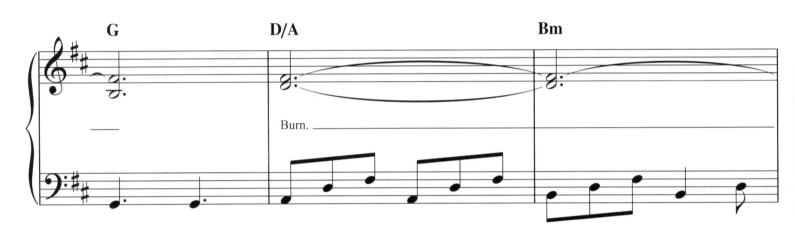

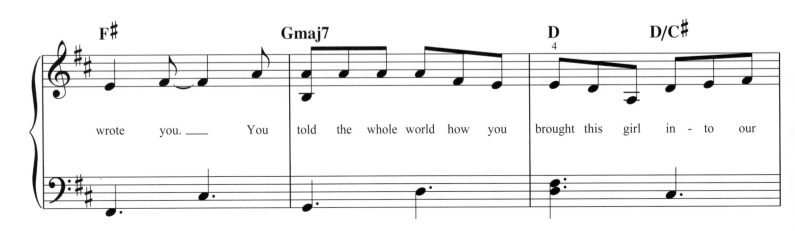

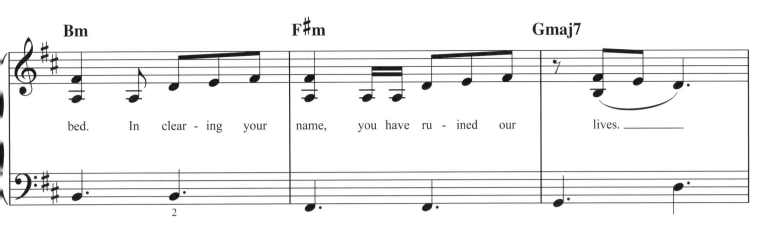

bed. In clear - ing your name, you have ru - ined our lives. _____

Do you know what An - gel - i - ca said

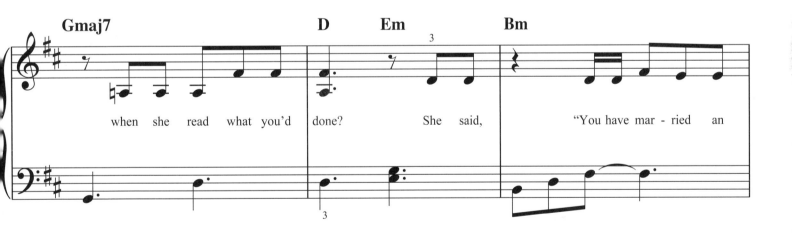

when she read what you'd done? She said, "You have mar - ried an

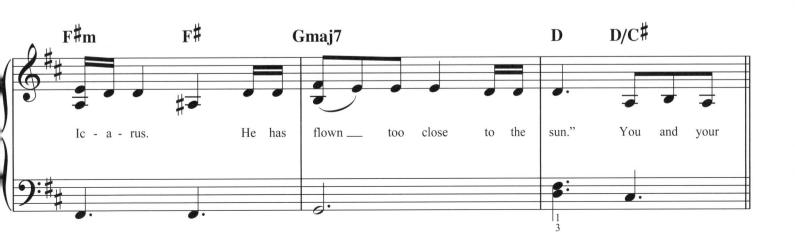

Ic - a - rus. He has flown ___ too close to the sun." You and your

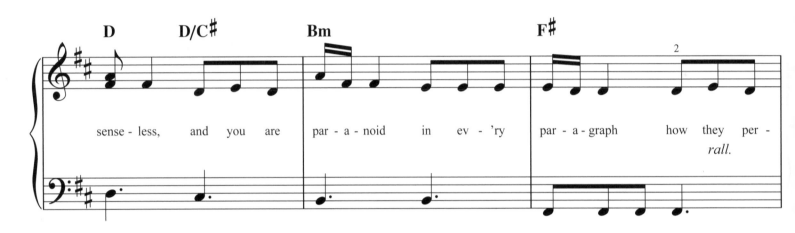

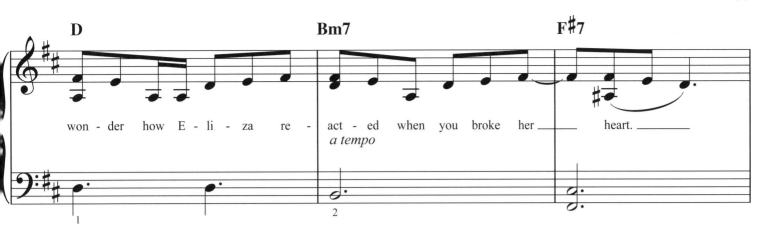

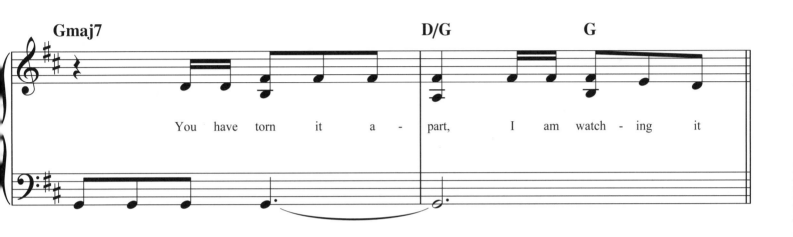

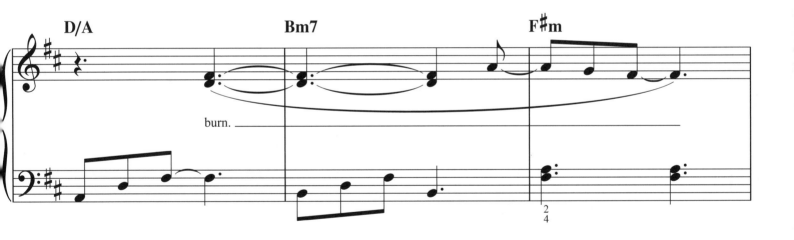

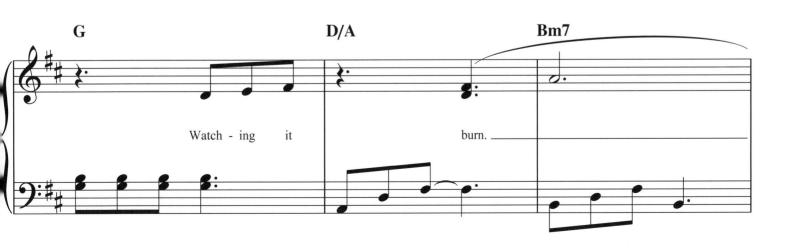

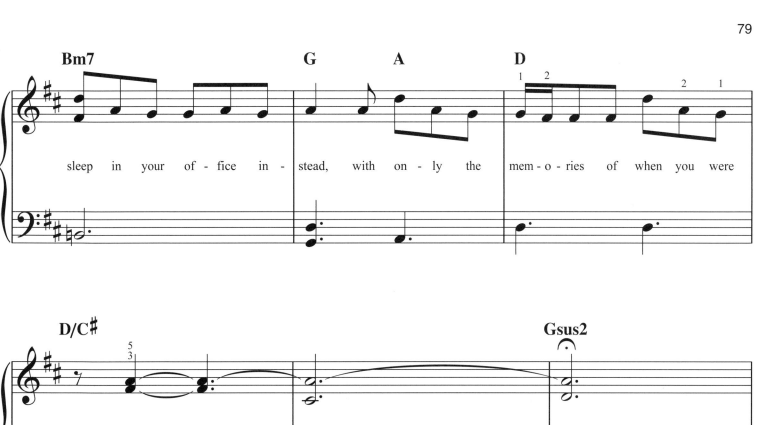

Bm7 · G · A · D

sleep in your of - fice in - stead, with on - ly the mem - o - ries of when you were

D/C# · Gsus2

mine. _____

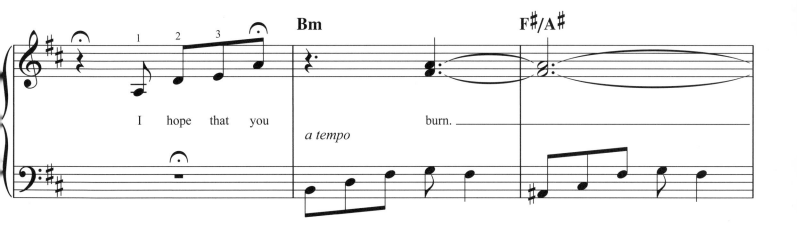

Bm · F#/A#

I hope that you

a tempo

burn. _____

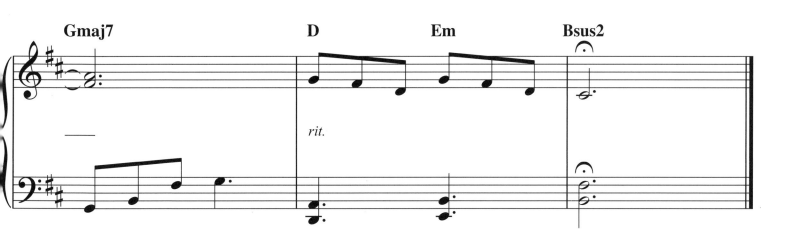

Gmaj7 · D · Em · Bsus2

rit.